The map of Antarctica can go any way you like. None points north.

The continent of Antarctica stretches across the bottom of the world, surrounded by a huge ice-strewn ocean and small islands. When people talk or write about 'the Antarctic' they usually mean the continent, the ice, the ocean and the islands. But there is no actual boundary to this enormous region. Generally people use 'the Antarctic' to mean everything south of the Antarctic Convergence. Sometimes they mean the area covered by the Antarctic Treaty only. You need to notice which boundary is being used when you hear or read about the Antarctic. This book is nearly all about the continent of Antarctica.

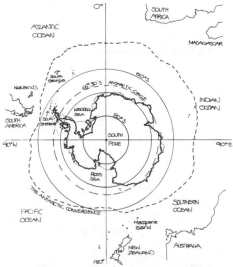

Explorers measured their journeys in Antarctic in nautical miles. One hundred nautical miles equal approximately one hundred and fifteen statute miles and one hundred and eighty-five kilometres. Nautical miles have been converted in this book to kilometres.

1

I grew up on the southern coast of Australia. The huge waves rolled on to the long empty beaches, and we knew that there was nothing except sea between us and the Antarctic.

My father showed me where glaciers had made deep scratches across the surface of rocks. But the glaciers were not travelling over the land and out to sea. They came the other way, out of the south.

My father was taught geology by the Antarctic explorer Sir Douglas Mawson. I used to look at the great waves, and think about their journey from the Antarctic. I stared at the sea and wondered about the glaciers grinding north over land no longer there.

So I have always wanted to find out about Antarctica. I have never visited it. But many of those who have, write so well about what they saw, and felt, and did, that it is easy to travel with them. A book like this depends on other people's research, and work. It is not possible to list the sources I have used; but if you want to read more about Antarctica there are excellent books to choose from.

I am very grateful to Dr Richard Laws, President of the Scientific Committee on Antarctic Research, and formerly director of the British Antarctic Survey, who kindly read the manuscript for me.

I would also like to thank the Librarians at the Scott Polar Research Institute in Cambridge and the Commonwealth Trust in London for their help.

MEREDITH HOOPER, LONDON 1991

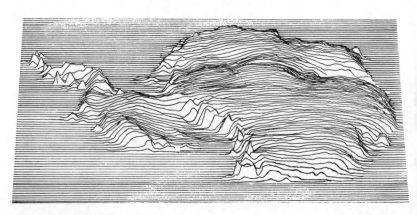

A _for_ ANTARCTICA

Facts and stories from the frozen South

Meredith Hooper

Illustrated by
Sally Townsend

Piccolo Books
A Piccolo Original

First published 1991 by Pan Books Ltd,
Cavaye Place, London SW10 9PG
9 8 7 6 5 4 3 2
ISBN 0 330 32240 0
© Meredith Hooper 1991
Phototypeset by Intype, London
Printed in England by Clays Ltd, St Ives plc

Acknowledgements

The author and publishers wish to thank the following for their kind
permission to reproduce photographs:

British Antarctic Survey for Crevasse in Nye Glacier – A Moyes; South
Pole surrounded by flags – C. W. M. Swithinbank; Aerial view of part
of Traverse Mountains – J. Paren.

Scott Polar Research Institute for Captain Scott's Polar party (18.1.1911)

Survival Anglia for Pancake ice; Adelie penguins on sea ice; Wandering
albatross; Krill; Weddell seal and new-born pup; Weddell seal and pup
at four weeks; Crabeater seals under tide crack; Leopard seal; Figures
with sledges on ice – Rick Price. Emperor penguins – Mike Tracey.
Husky; Husky team – Joel Bennett. Killer whale – Jeff Foott. Tabular
berg – Colin Willock. Ice shelf, Halley Bay – George Edwards.

Thanks also to Paul Aslin, formerly of the British Antarctic Survey, for
loan of his slides, photographs and other reference material for the
illustrations.

The author and publishers also wish to thank the Trustees of the
Mawson Estate, the University of Adelaide, and the editors Dr and Mrs
F. J. Jacka for permission to reproduce extracts from the book *Mawson's
Antarctic Diaries* (Allen & Unwin, Australia, 1988); and the Scott Polar
Research Institute, University of Cambridge, for permission to quote
from *Diary of the 'Terra Nova' Expedition to the Antarctic 1910–1912* by
Edward Wilson, © Scott Polar Research Institute 1972, published by
Blandford Press.

INTRODUCTION

Ice!

Dig down in Antarctica and you touch snow that fell before you were born.

Last year's snow hasn't melted in Antarctica. Nor the snow that fell the year before that. One hundred metres below the South Pole is snow that fell a thousand years ago. The weight of the snow above has turned it into clear bluey-green glacier ice.

Half a million years of snow covers Antarctica in huge white domes of ice. The ice sheets are one to four kilometres thick. Far, far below under the ice are the valleys, plains and hills of the continent. Sometimes the tops of mountains stick up in sharp rocky points.

The ice is so crushingly heavy it has altered the shape of our planet, flattening it at the South Pole. Deep down under the ice the rock of the continent has in places been pushed below the level of the sea. If all the ice melted, the continent would in time lift again. The world's oceans would fill with melt water until they rose sixty metres higher than they are now.

The ice sheets end at the coast in ice cliffs. Massive glaciers grinding down from the inland plateau spill out into the sea in great tongues of ice. Slabs of ice the size of small countries ride out over the sea in level ice shelves, trapping islands. Lumps of ice shelf break off and float away as icebergs. The edge of Antarctica is almost all made of ice. The sea around Antarctica is strewn with pieces of ice. In winter the sea freezes and the 'ice size' of the continent almost doubles.

Most of the world's ice is in Antarctica. Here, said one of the first scientists to visit the continent, is a living ice age. We think of the last ice age ending ten thousand years ago, but in the cold white world of Antarctica we can find out what an ice age is really like.

Antarctica – The Land

Antarctica stretches shapeless and lumpy across the bottom of maps. But look at our planet from a different angle. There is the continent of Antarctica, rather like a giant sting ray heading for the gap between Australia and southern Africa with a tail pointing to the tip of South America.

The Antarctic continent is one-tenth of all the world's land mass. It is the fifth largest continent, covering about fourteen million square kilometres. It is half as big again as the United States and fifty-six times bigger than the United Kingdom.

Antarctica is a long way from any other continent. A thousand kilometres separate the rugged tail – the Antarctic Peninsula – from South America. The next nearest continent, Australia, is two thousand five hundred kilometres away.

Antarctica has no national frontiers, no governments, no police. It's the highest, windiest, driest, coldest, wildest, iciest, cleanest, emptiest, quietest place on Earth.

The Antarctic continent is hostile and remote, isolated from the rest of the world by a stormy ocean, isolated from most living things by the extreme cold and harshness of its climate. It is a dangerous place to visit. Mistakes can't be made. It's rather like the ocean, or space. Antarctica makes the rules. The visitor needs to understand and obey them.

Antarctica: Who Named It?

A group of bright stars in the northern sky which can always be seen was given the name of Arctos, the Bear, by the ancient Greeks. The point around which all the stars seemed to turn was called the Arctic Pole. Some Greeks thought that the Earth was round. There must be land in the unknown southern half of the Earth to balance all the land they knew about in the northern half. They called the point opposite the Arctic Pole Antarktikos, which means 'opposite the Bear', opposite the north.

Antarctica: When Was It Found?

Many sailors searched for the 'Unknown South Land' which they thought must be somewhere south of the equator. Map makers drew the imaginary coastline of a huge continent filling the bottom of the world.

A few islands were discovered, and the large continent of Australia. Occasionally ships sailed far to the south into cold stormy seas where icebergs floated. Sometimes land was found covered in glaciers and snow. Were these new bits of land islands? Or were they part of the great southern continent? The idea of the continent was in people's minds. But it was very difficult to prove whether one really existed or not.

The British converted the warship HMS *Challenger* into a floating laboratory and sent her around the world to study the oceans. *Challenger* was the first steamship to cross the Antarctic Circle, on 16 February 1874. Rocks dredged up off the seabed here were later studied and found to be the kind of rocks which only come from a continent. Scientists decided that icebergs must have scraped the rocks off a continent on or near the South Pole. As the icebergs melted the rocks dropped into the sea. Here was proof.

By the beginning of this century everyone agreed that a continent existed although its shape wasn't known. Perhaps there were several large islands, or perhaps a doughnut-shaped land with sea in the middle. Pieces of coastline were marked in on maps which didn't join up with other bits.

The last blanks on the map of Antarctica were not filled in until the 1950s. No one could actually know what the continent really looked like until satellite pictures began being sent back from nine hundred and seventeen kilometres up in the sky, in the 1960s. Much of Antarctica is covered by cloud much of the time. Thousands of pictures had to be put together to get the final, clear, beautiful view of the continent.

Antarctica: Who Saw the Continent First?

We don't know. When sailors saw distant cliffs of ice they might have been looking at the continent without realizing it. Sometimes they saw immense icebergs which they thought must be land. Some discoveries turned out to be islands, but it was difficult to tell because solid ice joined islands to the mainland. In any case, no one knew what was actually there. So when a piece of land was seen, no one knew what it belonged to.

Britain, the United States, and Russia each claim that their sailors saw the Antarctic continent first, in 1820. The Russian Navy's Captain von Bellingshausen probably saw it on 27 January but he didn't say he did. The British naval officer Edward Bransfield said he saw it on 30 January. A nineteen-year-old American sailor, Nathaniel Palmer, said he saw it in November.

Antarctica: Who Landed on the Continent First?

'I jumped over the side of the boat,' wrote Carsten Borchgrevink, 'thus being the first man on shore.' 'I jumped ashore saying "I have the honour," ' wrote the Norwegian captain of the ship. 'I was the first out of the boat, to steady her,' said a New Zealand sailor. Whoever jumped first, the landing happened on 24 January 1895, at Cape Adare, Victoria Land.

The men were from the *Antarctic*, a Norwegian ship finding out if whales could be caught in the Ross Sea. The expedition was organized by Henryk Bull. Bull landed at Cape Adare as well, but he didn't join the argument. He just said he was happy to be among the first men to set foot on the real Antarctic mainland.

Probably none of them was first. Seventy-four years earlier, on 7 February 1821, an American sealer called John Davis sent a boat ashore to look for seals on what he said was a continent. Men hunting for seals usually kept quiet about where they went. Davis' diary was only discovered recently. Other sealers are likely to have landed as well, but we don't know their names.

ADÉLIE PENGUIN

Pebbles are precious to Adélie penguins. They fight over pebbles. They steal pebbles from each other. Pebbles are used to make nests. The best fighters and stealers have the biggest pile, and the highest nests. The penguin lies across the top of its pebble nest keeping the two eggs inside warm, and up out of the thick sludge of penguin droppings which covers the ground.

Each nest is just beyond pecking and stealing distance from the next. Large skua gulls with strong hooked beaks fly above the nests. Their dinners are under covers. But they don't waste time once a cover is lifted. If a penguin leaves its nest the eggs are gone.

Rocky shore is precious in Antarctica, because there isn't much. Almost all of the continent's coast is ice. During winter, snow covers everything. In summer the snow melts off a few rocky slopes leaving spaces where the little Adélie penguins can raise their chicks. Sometimes a summer blizzard blankets the penguin rookery, but the penguins keep sitting on their pebble nests under the snow.

Raising chicks in Antarctica is tough. The parents waddle to and from the sea bringing food. The chicks must grow from small balls of grey down to full-size birds with proper waterproof feathers during the few months of summer. If the winter ice starts coming back over the sea too quickly, and the journey for food takes too long, the chicks will die of hunger.

A well-fed chick looks like a floppy sack bulging with food. After a few weeks the chicks crowd together for safety while both parents work at food gathering. Somehow each parent coming back from days at sea finds its own chick, and aims a stream of half-digested food down the right throat. Some rookeries have tens of thousands of penguins. Penguins squabble and fight, and the chicks rush about. The noise is deafening, the smell and mess appalling. And still the skua gulls strut and swoop, attacking the penguins and feasting on weak or abandoned chicks.

By the end of summer the successful chicks have left for the sea. The weary adults stand on shore while their weatherworn, tatty old feathers fall out and new ones grow. They can't swim while this happens so they can't feed. Adélie penguins are seventy centimetres tall and weigh about five kilograms. After three weeks the handsome new coat has grown, but the exhausted, scrawny bird has lost half its weight.

Adélie penguins spend the winter out on the edges of the pack ice. In spring they start walking in single file over the ice towards their nesting sites. They walk between twenty and one hundred kilometres. They are about to begin the whole business of raising chicks again.

AGE

Knock a piece of lichen off a rock in Antarctica and you might have destroyed a thousand years of growth. Kill an Emperor penguin and you remove a creature which could have been born before the Second World War. The noisy brown skua gull flying around your head is probably thirty-five years old, as is the starfish on the seabed. The fish you would like to eat for breakfast has been alive for twelve years. Even the little krill, the centre of the Antarctic food chain, lives to be seven.

Many animals and plants in Antarctica have long lives compared to animals and plants in hot parts of the world. They grow slowly. They produce fewer offspring, with longer gaps between, and take great care of them. The harsh, cold conditions seem to slow down the life cycle. When animals and plants are destroyed more time is needed to replace them.

AIRCRAFT

The first aeroplane in Antarctica had no wings. The little open cockpit Vickers crashed on its trial flight in Australia, so Douglas Mawson took it to Antarctica in 1911 to pull loads like a tractor.

The first full-scale aeroplane flight was made on 20 December 1928, by Australian Sir Hubert Wilkins. He flew for eleven hours, two thousand one hundred kilometres along the Antarctic Peninsula in a Lockheed Vega monoplane, surveying and photographing Antarctica from the air.

The first flight over the South Pole was achieved on 28–29 November 1929 with American Richard Byrd as navigator. In fifteen hours fifty-one minutes the three-engined Ford flew from the Little America Base on the Ross Ice Shelf to the South Pole and back.

The first flight over the continent was made by American millionaire Lincoln Ellsworth in November 1935. With British pilot Herbert Hollick-Kenyon he flew his specially made metal monoplane from the Antarctic Peninsula to the Ross Sea, around three thousand seven hundred kilometres, landing four times on the inland snow.

Aircraft in Antarctica covered in a few hours distances which took explorers weary dangerous months. Pilots explored from the air. Aircraft could lift supplies, men, medical equipment – whatever was urgently needed – to where it was needed. Once aircraft began to be used in Antarctica the old way of exploring was changed, for ever. The first pilots felt guilty as they looked down at their friends slowly and painfully crossing the ice below.

But flying in Antarctica was dangerous. There were no charts, compasses didn't work properly, and controls could ice up fast. Weather changed quickly, and visibility disappeared in seconds. Once over the inland ice there were very few landmarks. The high cold air made it difficult for aircraft to gain height. Pilots had to be very skilled to land on unknown ice surfaces. The ice might look smooth but be covered in impossible hard high ridges. And if a plane was forced down there was nobody to help.

Today big transport planes fly equipment and people in from countries to the north on long and expensive flights. Small aircraft and helicopters are used in summer to fly scientists and equipment out to field work.

Airfields in Antarctica are a major problem. There isn't much flat land, and much of the ice-free land is used by wildlife for nesting and breeding. The American Base at McMurdo has an airport on the sea ice. Every few years it has to be shifted. The French have dynamited small islands off the coast for their airfield at Dumont D'Urville station, and the British have built a new airfield at Rothera off the Antarctic Peninsula. But many people fear that the easier it is to fly into Antarctica the more the continent is under threat.

REMOVING AN EGG FOR MEASUREMENT FROM WANDERING ALBATROSS' NEST

ALBATROSS

The wandering albatross is the world's largest ocean bird. Soaring and gliding on its three hundred and thirty centimetre wings, it feeds in the wild Southern Ocean.

Wandering albatross can live to be eighty years old, and they pair for life. Every two years the albatross pair return to the same nest site, on a northerly Antarctic island beyond the pack ice, to lay an egg. Both birds work hard to raise one chick through the long bitter winter. They often fly fifteen hundred kilometres from the nest searching for food for the down-covered chick.

No one knows what happens to a young wandering albatross once it has left its parents. It may stay at sea for several years, circling the world. But then it will come back to the island where it was born, and start looking for its life-time mate.

AMUNDSEN

Roald Amundsen had a plan. But almost no one knew about it. He wanted to be the first to reach the South Pole. Everyone thought he was going north to the Arctic in the famous polar ship *Fram*. But each piece of equipment he got ready – well-trained Greenland dogs, waterproof clothing, reindeer-fur suits, sledges, skis and ski boots, food, the prefabricated wooden hut – was for the south.

Everybody knew the British were trying to reach the South Pole. Commander Robert Scott journeyed for fifty-nine days towards the Pole in 1902 with two companions, Doctor Edward Wilson and Ernest Shackleton. Shackleton led his own expedition and nearly reached the Pole in 1908–9, finding a route up a glacier on to the high plateau. He and three companions turned back one hundred and seventy-nine kilometres from success, only just surviving an appalling journey. Now Scott was organizing a new expedition to leave in 1910, taking a large party because much scientific work was planned. But the Norwegian Amundsen had only one aim: to reach the Pole, first. If he wasn't first it wasn't worth doing. He concentrated everything on this decision: no science, no large party. And Amundsen had a great advantage. He knew he had a rival. Scott didn't.

Amundsen left Norway in the *Fram* on 9 August 1910. Each man on the expedition was used to outdoor work in the cold, and had valuable skills – cross-country skiing, dog-driving, carpentry. But the men were uneasy. Amundsen was an experienced explorer. He had travelled in the Antarctic and the Arctic where he lived with Eskimos and studied their survival techniques. Why was he sailing south with ninety-seven dogs? Why did he have a wooden hut on board, with a kitchen table and cooker?

Fram stopped at the island of Madeira in the Atlantic. Amundsen called the men together one hot, sticky afternoon. 'We are going to try to reach the South Pole,' he said. The men stared, in utter silence. They had joined an expedition for the opposite end of the world. You may leave if you wish, Amundsen told them. We will not stop again until we reach the Antarctic continent. Then we will race the English 'Hoorah!' shouted the champion skiier Olav Bjaaland. 'That means we will get there first.'

Why the secrecy? Amundsen had planned to be the first at the North Pole. But in September 1909 came the startling news that the North Pole had been reached. 'Why should anyone want to go to a place where somebody else has been?' said Amundsen. He decided to claim the South Pole. But he believed success depended on secrecy. He didn't want anyone stopping him because he had changed his plans.

Amundsen knew exactly where he wanted to build his base camp. That too was a secret. Scott and Shackleton had bases on Ross Island. A huge level shelf of ice stretched inland until it reached a range of mountains. The Pole was on the high plateau beyond the mountains. The British called the ice shelf the Barrier. It covered an area larger than France, and no one knew if it was afloat or part of the continent. But they knew that it moved, slowly, towards the sea, and that huge pieces of ice broke off and floated away as icebergs.

Amundsen decided to take a risk and build his own base actually on the ice shelf at a place called the Bay of Whales. This put him a little closer to the Pole than Scott, and already on the route. Scott had to move equipment on to the ice from Ross Island before he could start.

Amundsen landed on 14 January 1911. Scott had landed ten days earlier. But no one from Scott's expedition knew exactly where Amundsen was until February.

We underestimated Amundsen, said one of Scott's men later. Scott decided to carry on with his plans as if Amundsen had not arrived. Amundsen's plans had always included Scott. Amundsen intended to be first at the Pole, and felt he had as much right to try as anyone. After all he had been among the first men to winter in Antarctica, in 1895.

The wooden hut 'Framheim' was set into the ice a little way in from the sea. One and a half tonnes of supplies were carried part way along the route to the Pole and left in three depots. The nine men killed seals for fresh meat for themselves and the dogs. Then they settled in for the winter, working on their equipment – rebuilding sledges to save weight, improving ski boots, repacking food. The dogs had to pull everything to the Pole and saving weight was essential. Amundsen considered the dogs the most important part of the expedition. They were his transport, his engines. Success depended on their health and strength.

On 8 September 1911 the Norwegians set off. Amundsen was desperate about Scott. Had his rival already left? He was a man on the starting block who could not hear the starter's gun. But the weather was too harsh, and they were forced to turn back. They did not leave again until 19 October: four sledges, forty-eight dogs, five men – Amundsen, Bjaaland, Hassel, Helmer Hanssen, Wisting.

Amundsen was travelling a new route. Would they find mountains in their way? Scott was convinced dogs could not pull sledges up mountains. Amundsen was certain they could. On 17 November they reached the foot of high, wild mountains and began climbing, the dogs panting and clawing their way up dragging a tonne of equipment. In five days they had climbed over three thousand metres up a terrible glacier which they named the Axel Heiberg. The plan was now to shoot twenty-four of the weaker dogs, feed them to the others, and move as fast as possible across the plateau to the Pole. It was hard to kill the dogs. They had worked so well. But the remaining dogs were thin, and needed fresh food. 'When dog eats dog,' said Amundsen, 'only the teeth are left. And if they are very hungry, even these disappear.'

Travelling in thick fog and blizzards, amongst crevasses and glaciers, they struggled on until they reached the furthest south achieved by Shackleton. It was 8 December. The men's faces and hands were frost-bitten, the dogs were exhausted. Breathing was difficult in the high, cold air. Anxiously everyone searched the horizon for any sign of Scott. They talked about Scott, they worried, and fretted. Then at three in the afternoon on 14 December they stopped, in the flat white plain. They had reached the South Pole. They were the first.

Amundsen wanted no mistakes. Black marker flags were put up around the area of the Pole. A little tent with messages inside, and spare clothes and equipment, was set up on the place where they calculated the Pole to be. On the 17th they left. 'Farewell, dear Pole,' wrote Amundsen in his diary. 'I don't think we'll meet again.'

They had sixteen dogs and two sledges. They had plenty of food waiting in depots. They were fit.

These men understood snow, cold and ice. They were fine skiiers. Amundsen had worked for years at improving his techniques for Polar exploring. This had been a carefully planned journey, down to the last detail. With skis and dog teams the Norwegians could travel much further each day than the English, in fewer hours. Then men and dogs could rest. They needed to carry less food, and were able to avoid the colder weather at the end of the short summer season. Amundsen always said that if Shackleton had been equipped

with dogs, fur clothes, and skis, and understood how to use
them, he would have reached the Pole. Then, said Amundsen, he would not have come himself. There were difficulties
and dangers on the journey. But it had been brilliantly carried
out. Amundsen was a professional.

Early on Friday 25 January 1912 the five men saw the
chimneys of their hut poking above the snow. They had been
away for ninety-nine days, and travelled two thousand six
hundred and ten kilometres. The cook made hot cakes and
coffee. 'Have you been there?' the men in the hut asked.
'Yes, we've been there.' Everyone was safely back. This was
true happiness.

By 30 January the men, the surviving dogs, and the valuable equipment were on board ship. The door was closed on
a freshly cleaned hut. *Fram* sailed north to Australia. Reaching the Pole was one thing. But Amundsen wanted to be
first with the news, to be sure of the victory.

AMUNDSEN-SCOTT STATION

You can watch videos at the South Pole, eat hamburgers, have a
hot shower, have your teeth filled. The United States Government
built a permanent, fully equipped base here in 1957. Everything
to build the base was flown in and dropped by parachute. Some
did not open properly and things were smashed or buried in the
snow. The station sits in an area claimed by six nations. But the
United States does not recognize any claims to land in Antarctica.
The present station opened in 1972.

Long orange box-shaped buildings sit on the snow under a huge
shiny aluminium geodesic dome, fifty metres wide. Inside the
dome it's frosty cold, and the light is dim. Inside the orange
buildings it's warm and light. The fuel to keep the buildings
comfortable has to be flown in, like everything else at Amundsen-
Scott Station.

In summer more than fifty scientists and support staff live here.
The last plane flies out in mid February. The first relief plane will
not land till November. About twenty people stay at the South
Pole through the long dark winter.

ANIMALS ON LAND

You need a magnifying glass or a microscope to see most of Antarctica's land animals. They lurk amongst tufts of moss and on the undersides of stones. The continent's harsh climate, extreme cold, and lack of moisture mean the only land animals able to survive are tiny. Most are smaller than one millimetre.

Land animals can't escape for the winter. To prevent their cells from freezing and breaking like water pipes in houses some have special 'antifreeze' chemicals. Their body fluids stay liquid although the temperature drops far below zero.

Minute animals like mites, springtails, midges, nematodes, and tardigrades live in patches of lichen and moss, and on rock faces. Some live amongst the old feathers, broken eggs, and droppings of a penguin rookery, or the scraps of plants and seaweed in birds' nests. They eat microscopic fungi and algae, or each other.

The continent's largest land-living predator is a yellow mite around two millimetres long. It attacks and eats springtails half its size.

Most of the animals live on the Antarctic Peninsula, or along the coasts. But some mites have been found on rocks near the South Pole – the most southerly living creatures on Earth.

YELLOW MITE

ANIMALS ON THE SEA FLOOR

The Antarctic seems all ice, snow, and rock surrounded by cold ocean, a grey, white, and black world.

But go below the surface of the sea. An amazing number of strange and colourful creatures live on the sea floor. Pinky-red starfish, red and purple sea anemones, pale yellow coral, delicate sponges, fast-moving brittle stars, spiky orange sea spiders with ten or twelve legs, sea urchins, sea cucumbers and sea slugs live in the cold waters around Antarctica. Like other animals in Antarctica these creatures grow slowly in the cold. Some live a long time. Sponges can be two hundred years old, and limpets one hundred years.

Glaciers scrape rocks and silts off the Antarctic continent, and carry them slowly to the coast. Icebergs break off from the glaciers and carry all this material into the ocean. As the icebergs melt they drop their load of rock and debris. Every year five hundred million tonnes fall on the sea floor around Antarctica. The minerals dissolve to form rich supplies of food. Life is much easier to manage in the sea than on land. It's not nearly so cold in the water. So most life in Antarctica lives in the sea, or feeds from the sea.

But the sea floor has its dangers. In winter, ice grinds across it. The sea can freeze even on the sea bed. Icebergs bulldoze huge areas damaging everything. Many creatures move to deeper water in winter to avoid the ice.

ANTARCTIC CIRCLE

Nearly all of the Antarctic continent is within the Antarctic Circle, an imaginary line drawn around the Earth at latitude 66° 30' South.

North of the Antarctic Circle the sun rises once and sets once every day of the year – until we reach the Arctic Circle. Just south of the Antarctic Circle there is one day in the middle of winter when the sun never rises, and one day in the middle of summer when it never sets. The further south, the longer the night of winter lasts and the more days there are which have sunlight for twenty-four hours; until at the South Pole darkness lasts for half the year, and the sun rises once and sets once each year.

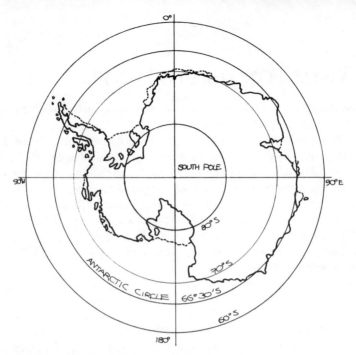

ANTARCTIC CONVERGENCE

Sailors heading south notice a sudden drop in the temperature of the sea. The air becomes much colder. To sailors this is the boundary of the Southern Ocean. From here on, they face wild, stormy seas and ice.

The Southern Ocean which surrounds the Antarctic continent is very cold. When this cold not very salty surface water flows north and meets warmer saltier water flowing south from the Atlantic, Indian and Pacific Oceans, the two waters mix together. The belt of mixing water loops and swirls around the world at about latitude 50° South. The mixture then sinks beneath the warm water and continues to slide slowly northward. This invisible boundary in the sea where the water temperature changes is called the 'Antarctic Convergence', or 'Polar Front'.

The boundary makes a useful way of describing the Antarctic regions. South of the boundary there is no plant even the size of a shrub. The creatures living south of the boundary are mostly different from those to the north. All the land and sea south of the Antarctic Convergence is usually called 'the Antarctic'. The continent itself is known as 'Antarctica'.

ANTARCTIC TREATY

The Antarctic Treaty is a unique international agreement. Governments decided to co-operate in Antarctica. They wanted to avoid conflict over this important part of the world. The Treaty has worked because people wanted it to work. Governments which claimed part of Antarctica, and those Governments which decided not to claim parts, agreed to 'freeze' the subject. Nothing done in Antarctica during the time of the Treaty would affect any nation's claims. Antarctica would be reserved for peaceful scientific work. All bases would be open to inspection. Scientific knowledge would be exchanged. No nuclear testing would be allowed. No military use would be made of Antarctica, although military personnel and equipment could help run bases. Decisions about Antarctica are made at meetings of the Treaty nations.

The Antarctic Treaty includes all land and ice shelves (but not sea) from 60° South. The Treaty took effect on 23 June 1961, with ways of changing it from 1991. Since the original twelve signatories, fourteen more countries have been added who have decided to be actively involved in Antarctic research, which gives them a role in making decisions. Another thirteen countries have agreed to abide by the terms of the Treaty. They have no vote at meetings. Nations representing eighty per cent of the world's population now support the Antarctic Treaty.

ARCTIC

The Arctic is an ocean surrounded by land. The Antarctic is land surrounded by ocean.

ARCTIC TERN

The Arctic tern flies from the Arctic to the Antarctic and back every year, a journey of forty thousand kilometres. This, the longest migration of any bird, means the Arctic tern spends eight months a year flying and almost all its life in daylight. As soon as it reaches the Antarctic it starts feeding on small creatures in the sea like krill. At the end of the Antarctic summer it flies back across the world to nest in the Arctic summer.

AURORA

The sky glows with wonderful colours. Lights flash and flicker, sweep upwards in great search-light beams, and hang in columns and fringes, or swinging swaying curtains. Men lie on the ice and watch, forgetting the cold, overwhelmed by the beauty. 'Curtains of fire would form, one above the other . . . real curtains suspended across the sky as if on invisible wires, and winding in and out in intricate folds. Pale green above, below they were banded with yellow, heliotrope and pink, while from end to end waves of intenser light raced in and out of the folds in a wild hide-and-seek, until the eye was dazzled.' (1911)

No one knew what caused an aurora. And at first no one could photograph it.

Antarctica is an excellent place to study our planet's upper atmosphere. Scientists now know that the aurora australis can reach from one hundred to one thousand kilometres up into the sky. They are caused by particles from the sun which come spiralling in towards Earth's magnetic poles, where they hit molecules of gas. The sky lights up like an enormous television screen. Aurorae can occur night after night.

There are plenty of photographs of aurorae now. But no picture can show their wonderful colour and beauty.

BACTERIA

Humans bring their bacteria with them to the Antarctic. And everything done by humans – and their animals – is preserved in the cold. Manure made by Scott's ponies in 1911 is still somewhere in the ice, and the bacteria in it are surviving.

The Antarctic is a very clean place. Humans hardly touched it until this century. The early explorers felt they were free from the usual diseases of civilization.

BALLOON

The higher you go the further you can see. Even climbing a tree gives a better view. But there were no trees to climb in Antarctica. Two explorers tried to explore using balloons.

On 4 February 1902 a big limp balloon, a wicker basket, and cylinders of hydrogen were unloaded from Commander Scott's ship *Discovery* on to the ice. The balloon was inflated and Scott rose into the air. Eagerly he looked south for the first real view inland. He saw an enormous, unchanging level white surface stretching away as far as the eye could see. One more ascent was made – then all the gas cylinders were used up.

On the other side of the continent, on the sea ice, a German expedition inflated their balloon on 29 March. The leader, Professor Drygalski, rose five hundred metres and stared at the distant mainland. He stayed up for two hours taking photographs and describing what he could see to the men on his ship below, by telephone.

BASES

Humans migrate to Antarctica for the summer. Like birds and whales they come south from many different places. Every summer over five thousand people live in Antarctica. But once the last plane flies out in autumn, and the last ship leaves, anyone still in Antarctica must stay until the following spring. There are usually a thousand 'over-winterers'.

People live in Antarctica in bases or scientific stations. Some buildings perch on little scrapings of rock surrounded by glaciers. A few are on bare islands just off the coast. Several sit in ice shelves with only ventilator shafts and antennas sticking above the surface. There are a few bases inland on the ice sheet, and some on rocky beaches among the nesting sites of penguins. The bases cling on against the wind and cold, the ice and the loneliness.

Buildings in Antarctica have to be able to survive a tremendously hostile climate. Some of the bases are very simple, rather like mountain huts or barracks. Some, like the American base at McMurdo, are small towns where people can be 'protected' from Antarctica outside, if they wish, and experience little bits of home.

There are about thirty year-round bases in Antarctica, plus more which open for the summer. Most have scientists working on various projects. Some do very little science at all. Many have members of armed forces helping run them.

Bases need replacing. Most are on rock, but buildings on ice give off heat and slowly sink. The ice moves, dragging buildings along and down. Snow drifts against any object which sticks up, and never melts, gradually covering buildings. Five bases were built one after the other on the Ross Ice Shelf at 'Little America'. All sank into the ice and were crushed. The Russians and Argentinians built stations on the Filchner Ice Shelf. An enormous piece of the Ice Shelf broke off in 1986 and the two bases, fortunately with no one inside, floated out into the Weddell Sea.

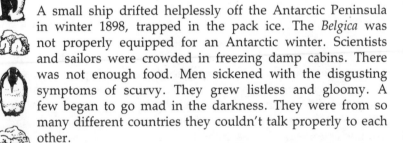

BELGICA

A small ship drifted helplessly off the Antarctic Peninsula in winter 1898, trapped in the pack ice. The *Belgica* was not properly equipped for an Antarctic winter. Scientists and sailors were crowded in freezing damp cabins. There was not enough food. Men sickened with the disgusting symptoms of scurvy. They grew listless and gloomy. A few began to go mad in the darkness. They were from so many different countries they couldn't talk properly to each other.

No one knew if the leader of the expedition meant to let the ship be frozen in. Adrien de Gerlache was a young Belgian naval officer who raised just enough money to get his expedition to Antarctica, but not enough to equip it properly. He wanted to carry out scientific work with an international crew. He did discover islands off the coast of the Antarctic Peninsula. But then the nightmare of the winter took over. The first Antarctic winter spent by an exploring ship was a disaster.

After almost thirteen months the ship finally got free. The

hair of a young Norwegian on board, Roald Amundsen, turned grey during the winter. But he had learned many important lessons about survival which he would use when he led his own expedition south twelve years later.

BELLINGSHAUSEN

The Russians decided to explore both ends of the Earth at the same time in 1819. They sent one expedition north and another south to make discoveries 'as close as possible to the South Pole'.

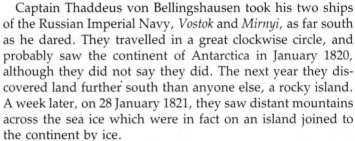

Captain Thaddeus von Bellingshausen took his two ships of the Russian Imperial Navy, *Vostok* and *Mirnyi*, as far south as he dared. They travelled in a great clockwise circle, and probably saw the continent of Antarctica in January 1820, although they did not say they did. The next year they discovered land further south than anyone else, a rocky island. A week later, on 28 January 1821, they saw distant mountains across the sea ice which were in fact on an island joined to the continent by ice.

Bellingshausen got back home to Russia in August 1821 after two years away. Little notice was taken of his great expedition. The Russians had nothing more to do with the Antarctic until they set up scientific bases in the 1950s.

BERGY BITS

Bergy bits are huge chunks of broken up or melted iceberg, or pieces of ice which have dropped off a glacier, the size of a house.

They roll backwards and forwards, floating deep in the sea with cracks and holes and air bubbles escaping as they melt.

BIRDS

Millions of sea birds come to the Antarctic every summer to feed during the long hours of daylight on the rich supplies of food in the sea. Their real problem is finding land to nest on. Some nest around the coast of the continent. Some nest on islands beyond the reach of the pack ice. Huge numbers of birds crowd into the same nesting sites.

The millions of birds are made up of only a few species. Sea birds breeding south of the Antarctic Convergence are albatross, penguins, petrels, tern, skuas, gulls, and the big blue-eyed shag.

BLACK

White ice and snow reflect heat. Black absorbs heat. Rocks in Antarctica get warm in summer, causing nearby snow and ice to melt.

All through the winter of 1902 the German ship *Gauss* was trapped in thick pack ice. Spring came, and the ice began to break up, but not the floe which held the ship. The scientists on board tried blasting the six-metre thick ice with explosives, they tried cutting it with steel saws. Then the leader of the expedition, Professor Drygalski, noticed that soot from the ship's funnel had settled on the ice and made it mushy. That gave him an idea.

A trail of black coal ash was laid across the white ice to a distant stretch of open water. All dark-coloured rubbish was added – penguin blood, rotten food. As the sun shone the ice melted under the rubbish. Within a month there was a two-metre deep trench. In February 1903 the ice floe started breaking along the line of the trench, and they were free.

BLIZZARD

Describe a blizzard as a strong wind with falling or blowing snow and it doesn't sound too terrible. But Antarctic blizzards are very dangerous. Outside work must stop. You can get lost three foot-steps away from your door. All sense of direction goes in the numbing whirling whiteness and the deafening roar of wind. The snow is fine, like dust, or powder. It plasters up your eyes and ears and fills your mouth and nose. It feels like a bad attack of asthma. Your brain feels bewildered, numbed.

A blizzard can come within minutes and last for days, at any time of the year.

BLUBBER

Blubber acts like a coat, or an envelope, stopping the heat from leaving a warm-blooded animal's body. It is a layer of fat just under the skin, ten centimetres thick in a seal, much thicker in a whale. Penguins' blubber makes them heavy, but as they don't fly it doesn't matter.

Blubber is full of oil. Seals, whales and penguins were all hunted for the oil in their blubber. It was used for a large number of things: lighting buildings, making margarine, tanning fine leathers, and lubricating in high pressures and temperatures.

Men living in the Antarctic used chunks of blubber as fuel in specially designed blubber stoves. It burnt with a fierce heat making lots of black soot. Hungry men ate cooked blubber. Really hungry men ate it raw. When you bit on a juicy piece of blubber the oil spurted in all directions into your mouth. 'It was hard at first to get used to,' said one explorer. 'But we did.'

BLUE WHALE

A blue whale is as long as a ten-storey building is high. It weighs the same as twenty-five male elephants. Its heart is the size of a small car. A child could wriggle down its main arteries. Its baby is born weighing three tonnes and drinks six hundred litres of milk a day. The blue whale is the largest creature alive, and the largest ever to have lived.

Yet the blue whale feeds mainly on one of the smaller sea creatures, the six centimetre-long krill. Krill eat the smallest plants in the sea. So the food chain goes with very few moves from the smallest to the largest. A blue whale swallows around four tonnes of krill a day.

Every summer blue whales have come to Antarctica to eat krill. As the massive blue whales surface to breathe they blow out a mixture of air, water vapour, oil, and mucus which smells strongly of oil and fish. The blows were very high, said an explorer, and looked almost like smoke from factory chimneys.

'One sees first a small, dark bump appear and then immediately a jet of grey fog squirted upwards . . . up rolls an immense blue grey . . . round back . . . and then the whole sinks and disappears.'

The chance of seeing blue whales in the Antarctic today is very small. At the beginning of this century whalers began killing them for the oil in their blubber, and the 'whalebone' in their mouths. There were probably two hundred thousand blue whales. Now there are only a few thousand left.

BORCHGREVINK

Carsten Borchgrevink scored a lot of firsts. He led the first party of men ever to live on the Antarctic continent, and the first to spend the long dark winter on land. He was the first to take dogs to the Antarctic.

Borchgrevink pioneered many ways of exploring in Antarctica but no one took much notice. He wasn't liked. People in England were annoyed because he got in first. A big British expedition was being organized, to be led by Captain Scott. This, people thought, should get all the attention and money. But Borchgrevink was determined to lead a scientific expedition and he persuaded a British publisher to pay for him.

Borchgrevink was a Norwegian, with a British mother, who had emigrated to Australia. All but five of his 'British Antarctic Expedition 1898–1900' were Norwegian. The ten men chosen to live ashore at Cape Adare for the winter of 1899 arrived on a dark gloomy day. The ship's decks were covered in frozen sea water. The coast seemed terrible, wild and desolate. Two prefabricated wooden huts were put up on the only possible place, a stony beach. Millions of penguins nested here in the summer and the smell was awful.

Gales and blizzards hammered the huts. Huge blocks of ice were forced up on to the beach, and the roaring and crushing sound of the ice at sea was appalling. No one knew how men would cope crammed together in the cold and darkness of an Antarctic winter. 'We got very sick of each other's company,' said Borchgrevink. 'We knew each line in each other's faces. Each one knew what the other one had to say. . . . The silence roared in our ears.'

One summer morning their ship came back for them. As a boy Borchgrevink read the famous British Antarctic explorer James Clark Ross who in 1841 had discovered this area. Now he was exploring the Ross Sea. Borchgrevink and his men were the first to climb the mysterious ice cliffs seen by Ross, and travel inland on the icy surface.

Borchgrevink left a great deal of equipment and rubbish at Cape Adare. Captain Scott's expedition stopped here in 1901. Men poked amongst the piles and collected useful things. This first settlement by humans on the continent started a tradition of leaving mess behind.

BRASH ICE

Brash ice are the smallest bits of ice floating in the sea, the wreckage of all other forms – decayed remains of an iceberg, all that's left after pack ice breaks up, the bits that fall off a glacier. They are pieces of sea ice smaller than two metres across.

BRUCE

William Bruce was a Scot who loved Scotland, science and exploring. He combined all three loves in a Scottish Antarctic expedition which spent the winter of 1903 on Laurie Island, north of the Antarctic Peninsula. A stone hut and a wooden magnetic observatory were built, and Bruce and his fellow scientists studied the weather, the sea, plant and animal life, and rocks. In spring they cut and blasted their ship, the *Scotia*, free, and discovered a new coast on the continent which they named Coats Land after their Scottish sponsors.

BRUCE'S SHORE PARTY OUTSIDE OMOND HOUSE, LAURIE ISLAND

The British Government refused to take over Bruce's meteorological base at Laurie Island. But the Argentinians agreed to. It is the oldest permanently inhabited base in the Antarctic region. The Argentinians call it Orcadas.

BURIED CONTINENT

The Antarctic continent is buried under ice and snow. What does it really look like? Scientists have worked out ways of probing down to the hidden land. Radar signals sent out from aircraft and satellites pass through the ice and are reflected off the rock deep below. The time taken for the signals to go down and back reveals the shape of the land and the depth of the ice.

Remote-sensing techniques like this reveal a very rugged landscape. Mountain ranges as high as the Swiss Alps are hidden beneath the ice. There are deep troughs far below sea level. Antarctica is not after all a single continent. If all the ice was removed, Lesser or West Antarctica which includes the Antarctic Peninsula would be a group of islands. Greater or East Antarctica bounded by the Transantarctic Mountains would be mostly above sea level.

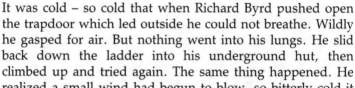

BYRD

It was cold – so cold that when Richard Byrd pushed open the trapdoor which led outside he could not breathe. Wildly he gasped for air. But nothing went into his lungs. He slid back down the ladder into his underground hut, then climbed up and tried again. The same thing happened. He realized a small wind had begun to blow, so bitterly cold it closed his breathing passages. The thermometer that morning had read – 71°C. Even lying in his sleeping bag reading a book he froze his finger.

The wind grew into a blizzard. Byrd knew he was safe in his hut. Only the stove chimney and air ventilators stuck up above the snow, and some meteorological instruments which measured the weather. Once he went up to check them. The night was so dark he couldn't see his hand. The light from his torch stopped where it began. Walking three steps through the rushing snow was like pushing through heavy surf.

The wind direction indicator stopped working, and Byrd decided he must try to mend it. Heaving the trapdoor open he crawled out into blinding smothering blizzard. The wind screeched and hammered. Millions of tiny stinging snow pellets exploded against his face, and clogged his nostrils and mouth. The wind roared with appalling noise. The great ice shelf in which his hut was buried seemed to shake and groan.

Byrd let the trapdoor fall shut. He didn't want the tunnel below filling with drifting snow. Crawling to the instrument he realized he couldn't fix it. He crawled back to the trapdoor.

It was already buried in snow. Scraping around with his mittens, Byrd pulled at the door handle. It didn't give. He heaved with all his strength. Nothing.

Byrd panicked. He clawed at the trapdoor, hitting it with his fists. He pulled at the handle until his hands were too weak from cold to do any more. Below him was safety: heat, warmth, food. And he was above, shut out. He could do nothing. Byrd lay over the frozen door. 'You damn fool,' he kept saying, over and over. 'You damn fool.'

The blizzard beat at him, a solid wall of pounding snow. It felt like an enemy, attacking only him, shaking his brains inside his head, taking his air, blocking his vision. Half-frozen, Byrd reached out in the darkness and found the round, cold metal air ventilator sticking out of the roof of his hut. He looked down through it. A faint patch of light showed on the floor far below. A small patch of warmth rose up, and touched his face.

The warmth and light helped him think. Perhaps he could wrench the ventilator pipe out and use it as a tool to dig with. But the pipe wouldn't budge. His arms ached. How long had he been outside? He had no idea. How long could he survive the cold? Then he remembered. A week ago he had left a shovel somewhere, stuck in the snow. If only he could find it! He lay down, holding on to the pipe, and felt around with his feet. No luck. Creeping blindly to the trapdoor he again felt around with his feet. He dared not let go of something familiar or he would get lost. His foot knocked against the other ventilator pipe, and edging across to it, he hung on and kicked with his feet. This time his ankle hit the shovel handle.

Byrd inched back to the trapdoor. Using the shovel as a lever, he managed to wrench the door open with his shoulder. He rolled down the shaft, and tumbled in to the light and warmth of the room.

The stove had blown out. Byrd pulled his clothes off and hoisted himself, exhausted, into bed.

Admiral Richard Byrd was living alone in the silence, darkness, and bitter cold of an Antarctic winter. His home was a small hut which he could cross in three steps, and two tunnels dug in the ice and piled with stores. But he was more than alone. He could not leave and he could not be rescued. His hut was the first building ever made in the interior of Antarctica. Byrd was living in a hole in the great flat empty expanse of the Ross Ice Shelf.

No one had ever observed and measured the winter weather inland in Antarctica. Byrd believed it needed to be done. The little hut did not have enough supplies for three men, and Byrd thought two men would get on each other's nerves. He had been in Antarctica before, leading an expedition which achieved the first flight over the South Pole. Now on this second expedition he had decided to take the risk of living in the inland hut by himself. He could contact his men at base camp two hundred kilometres away on the edge of the Ross Sea by radio. The only dangers he could think of were fire, getting lost and becoming ill. But he was an experienced explorer, used to danger. And he wanted to try the challenge of living alone through the world's worst weather.

Nine days after the near disaster of the blocked trapdoor, on the last day of May 1934, Byrd was talking by radio with the base at Little America. It was his seventieth day alone. Winter wasn't half-way through. Outside not even a streak of red sky showed at midday. Black night lasted all twenty-

four hours. The engine powering the radio sounded faulty and Byrd went into the ice tunnel where he kept it to check. The air was thick with fumes from the exhaust. Byrd bent over the engine to adjust it, and collapsed, unconscious.

Byrd nearly died. The engine was giving off poisonous carbon monoxide. So was the oil-burning stove which warmed his hut, melted ice for water, and cooked his food. It takes a long time to recover from carbon monoxide poisoning. Yet Byrd had to use the stove, to say alive.

He suffered agonizing illness. Existence in the hut was almost unbearable. For many days at a time he was too weak to look after himself. He used the stove as little as possible. Ice crept up the walls of his filthy hut towards the ceiling. But slowly, painfully, he managed to keep the meteorological measurements going, and stay in radio contact with base camp. He hid his illness from his men. He was expedition leader, and he knew a rescue attempt in the middle of winter was impossible.

On his first expedition to Antarctica in 1928–30 Byrd used aircraft successfully. Now in this second expedition in 1933–35, he was trying motor vehicles – four tractors and two snowmobiles. The Citroën tractors managed to get through to him in August, and save his life.

Byrd was an American hero and everything he did was news. His journeys to Antarctica made Americans interested in this extraordinary, remote place. Parts of the continent were claimed for the United States, although the government did not make the claims formal.

CATS

Most ships have a ship's cat. Cats are great favourites with sailors. But cats left ashore on islands around Antarctica have caused a disaster. Just two cats were left on Marion Island in 1949. Now their wild descendants kill half a million birds annually. A million and a quarter birds are killed each year on Kerguelen Island by the descendants of cats which arrived in the 1950s.

Cats cannot survive in the wild on the Antarctic continent. But they have visited, on board ship. As HMS *Terror* sailed along the coast in 1842 a small fish froze to the bow. The fish was lifted on board inside a block of ice. The ship's surgeon was excited. Perhaps this was a new species, and he would be the discoverer. But before he could study the fish the ship's cat ate it up.

CHARCOT

Dr Jean-Baptiste Charcot had his own ship, the *Français* which he planned to take to the Arctic. Then news came that a Swedish expedition was in trouble in the Antarctic. Charcot changed his plans and decided to go south and search for the explorers. He asked the people of France for money, and his journey turned into a national expedition. He was to explore, do scientific work, and find out if Antarctica was a continent or several large islands.

Charcot reached South America and heard that the Swedish under Otto Nordenskjöld were safe. He sailed on south. 'Very little exploration has been done,' he said. 'We have only to get there to achieve something great and fine.'

Five national expeditions were in Antarctica at this time: German, Swedish, English, Scottish, and French. Charcot spent the winter of 1904 at an island, then crossed the Antarctic Circle in the spring. His exploration of the Antarctic Peninsula was considered a success, and he returned to France a hero.

The government paid for a second expedition. His new ship *Pourquoi-Pas?* was modern and comfortable. She even had electric lights. Again Charcot spent the winter at an island, then explored south along the Peninsula in spring 1909. His ship ran on to rocks – which had also happened on the first expedition – causing serious damage. But Charcot went on exploring, making charts, and discovering new land.

CLAIMS TO TERRITORY

Ceremonies for taking possession of parts of Antarctica were very quick. Finding somewhere to land wasn't easy. It was too cold to stand around. Usually men rowed to a rocky island, stood amongst the penguins, said the words, and rowed back to their ships fast. Most explorers 'took possession' of what they thought they had discovered on behalf of their governments back home. Later some new methods of laying claim to a territory were tried. The Germans threw long aluminium darts out of flying boats over inland Antarctica in 1939. There are flags and tins with statements claiming land on behalf of various countries dotted around the continent.

Governments began officially declaring that parts of Antarctica belonged to them this century. Who took what, for what reason and how is very complicated. Nations started to compete with each other for the frozen continent. Lawyers argued fiercely, and still do. Historians got involved, because who first saw a piece of land, or who first carried out a ceremony of taking possession, seemed important. Names given to geographical features were argued about, because that might help somebody's claim.

By the 1940s Antarctica was divided up into wedges like a pie. Australia, France, New Zealand, and Norway had separate slices. Britain, Argentina, and Chile disagreed about overlapping slices, which included the Antarctic Peninsula. The Americans, Belgians, Germans, Japanese, and Russians said that they had claims which they had not taken up. The Americans and Russians say they will not recognize anybody else's claims. A big wedge was left unclaimed. All discussions and arguments about ownership and possession were put aside by the Antarctic Treaty of 1961.

Some things are thought to help the claims for territory in spite of the Treaty. Various countries run Post Offices. Argentina and Chile moved families with children into bases. Many scientific stations have been set up to 'establish a presence', which means 'be there'. Lawyers think that living in a place continuously helps with a claim to own it.

CLOTHES

A naked human body can survive for a few minutes in Antarctica's cold. But humans need layers of clothes, like an artificial shell, when temperatures stay below freezing. The body is a bit like a fire. It gives out heat. Clothes trap air, insulating the body and keeping its heat. They stop the wind from chilling the body below the level of safety. Layers of loose, light-weight clothes are best.

People living in Antarctica today wear normal underclothes with long-sleeved, long-legged thermal underwear rather like pyjamas on top. They wear a woollen shirt and sweater, and two pairs of trousers. Wind-proof cotton anorak and trousers are worn in the open air with Velcro strips because wind can get through the holes in zips. Heads, hands, and feet need special attention. Clothes are made of synthetic material as well as wool and cotton. Of course when the sun shines it can be warm enough to work in shirtsleeves.

The first men in the Antarctic piled on whatever they had – Army greatcoats, human-hair socks, woolly scarves, felt hats, tweed jackets. The men on Scott's expedition 1910–12 were very grateful because the New Zealand government gave them a hundred and thirty grey woollen pullovers. Jaeger underwear made of wool was popular. Burberry windproof jackets, trousers, and leggings made of a special fine-woven cotton were essential. Wives and aunts knitted to keep their men warm – balaclavas, mittens, and a special 'body-warmer' for one scientist which went from the armpits to the top of his legs, held up with shoulder straps.

Clothes got torn and worn out and filthy dirty. Men had to make do with what they had, mending and patching. It was almost impossible to dry clothes when out on an expedition, and difficult enough back in a crowded hut with little heat.

Amundsen studied what Eskimos wore, and among other clothes supplied his men with suits of reindeer-skin on the Eskimo pattern. He knew that Eskimos wore their clothing loose to allow air to circulate and sweat to escape. But most Europeans closed the edges of their clothing to keep out the cold and snow. As they worked, their bodies sweated. The sweat, unable to evaporate, froze between the layers of clothing. At night, as men warmed up in their sleeping bags the ice melted and soaked their clothes and bags. In the morning it froze again. Clothes got heavier, damper, and colder, and the men more miserable. There wasn't enough fuel to warm the tent and dry the clothes. Today great care is taken to let clothes 'breathe' and sweat escape.

MODERN ANTARCTIC EXPLORATION CLOTHING

CLOTHING FROM 1903

The Eskimo anorak or parka included a hood. Most of the men who had wind-proof tops made to the Eskimo design had separate hoods. As a result they lost heat around their necks, and the wind and snow had another place to work its way in to their cold bodies.

COAL

On the way to the South Pole Scott and his men discovered coal in the mountains. Millions of years ago trees grew here, and layers of plant material turned slowly into coal. But the large supplies of coal in the Transantarctic Mountains are of poor quality.

COASTLINE

Antarctica does not have a friendly coastline. Almost all of the thirty-two thousand kilometres is ice – glaciers, floating ice shelves, or ice cliffs. Only five per cent is rock. Much of the coast has been ground down well below the level of the sea by icebergs. The continental shelf is three hundred metres deeper than in all other continents, because the weight of ice has pushed the entire land down.

Ice covers much of the sea close to shore even in summer. It is difficult to tell where Antarctica begins and ends, what is ice and what is continent.

COOK

Captain James Cook was sent to discover, once and for all, if a great continent existed anywhere in the southern ocean. He sailed south until vast fields of pack ice stopped him; then he worked along the edge of the ice looking for a way in. Three times he took his men south amongst the dangerous icebergs and fog, the decks and sails heavy with ice, the men half starved and half frozen.

Cook sailed in a great circle further south than anyone had ever been. He did find desolate islands with massive glaciers. But he found no continent. He reckoned that there must be an ice-covered land further to the south, near the Pole. Where else could all the ice in the sea come from? But he had to give up the search and turn for home. The expedition lasted three years, 1772–75, and Cook's two small ships *Resolution* and *Adventure* were the first, as far as we know, to cross the Antarctic Circle (17 January 1773).

'I . . . had ambition,' wrote Cook after he returned home, 'not only to go farther than anyone had been before, but as far as it was possible for man to go.' The ice had stopped him. Cook thought the lands they had discovered were horrible: bleak, frozen and savage. Land even further south would be terrible indeed. Perhaps no one would ever be able to get there.

We now know that James Cook was exploring when the world's temperatures were lower than they are today, perhaps by 1.5°C, and the ice conditions were worse.

CRABEATER SEALS

Crabeater seals don't eat crabs, they eat krill which swarm in the Antarctic seas. The seals strain the krill through their specially evolved five-lobed teeth.

Crabeaters live out in the drifting pack ice within easy reach of the krill. But this puts them within easy reach of the hungry leopard seal which eats young crabeater pups as they try the water. Most crabeaters have terrible scars on their skins from the teeth of leopard seals. All crabeaters – and the leopard seals – are possible meals for the dangerous killer whale which hunts in packs through the ice. If a crabeater survives being a meal it might live to be forty years old.

Each crabeater family – a male, a female, and a pup – lives on a floating piece of ice in the summer, separate from the next. The baby grows enormously fast. In four weeks it is more than four times its birth weight, and looking after itself.

In the past no one knew how many crabeaters there were because the pack ice covers a huge area of ocean and is very difficult to get into. Now, with helicopters and icebreakers, vast numbers of crabeaters have been discovered. They are the most populous seal on Earth – there are somewhere between fifteen and thirty million of them.

CREAN

Leaders of expeditions are remembered. But ordinary members of expeditions are often forgotten. Many were brave, tough, resourceful men. Their work was vital. And they had amazing adventures.

Here are some of the adventures of Tom Crean, of the Royal Navy, who arrived in Antarctica by chance. As Scott's ship was leaving New Zealand for the Antarctic in 1901 a sailor was killed. Crean, a tall well-built Irishman, came on board as replacement.

Crean came south again with Scott on his second expedition. Late in February 1911 Crean and two other men were crossing the sea ice with four sledges and four ponies.

In the night they woke to find themselves floating out to sea. The floe had split under the ponies, drowning one. The floe split again but luckily everyone was on the same piece. The ponies were vital for Scott's plans to get to the South Pole. The men jumped the animals from one piece of rocking, slippery ice to the next, dragging the sledges after them, as the lumps of ice jostled in the freezing water. The ice was breaking up fast. Killer whales raced up and down in the cracks between the ice, eating seals. After six hours the three men scrambled on to a strong-looking floe. Crean offered to try to reach land, and find help.

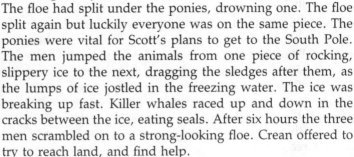

The others watched Crean judging the movement of the ice pieces as they heaved in the freezing water, swung towards each other and swept apart. The killer whales kept rearing up their great heads and staring as Crean jumped across the seething ice. Hour after hour Crean worked at finding a place where he could leap on to the ice cliff then scramble up it. One false move and he was finished. But he managed it, and set off across the snow to find help. But in spite of tremendous effort only one pony was saved.

Eleven months later Crean was two hundred and seventy-eight kilometres from the South Pole. Scott ordered him to turn back, with fellow seaman William Lashly and Lieutenant 'Teddy' Evans. Scott took their fourth companion, Bowers, to strengthen his own sledging party.

Crean, Lashly and Evans had been pulling their sledge for ten weeks. Weary and hungry they turned for the long, dangerous journey home. They said their hard goodbyes to the men who were going on to the Pole and gave three cheers. They kept looking back until Scott and his four companions were black dots in the distant whiteness, heading south.

Each day was a battle to cover a punishing distance, and a battle against hunger. After three weeks Evans began to sicken with scurvy. He struggled on but Crean and Lashly had to do most of the camping, cooking, and the back-breaking hauling of the sledge. Three weeks later Evans collapsed. Crean and Lashly tied the sick man to the sledge and dragged him. Fifty-six kilometres from an outpost hut where there was a chance of help, Evans could go no further. Lashly and Crean could have left Evans, to save their own lives. But Lashly looked after him in the tent, and Crean set off. If anything happened to Crean – if he slipped into a crevasse, or lost his way – if a blizzard came down, or he was too weary to keep walking – nothing could save him.

Tom Crean walked for eighteen hours. His only food was three biscuits and two sticks of chocolate. Back in the tent Lashly kept Evans alive. Unless help came quickly Evans would die. Then Lashly would die, because their food was almost finished.

But Crean reached the hut, and found someone there. Best of all, it was the doctor. Half an hour after he arrived a blizzard began and it was impossible to see. His survival was that close. They were able to get back to the tent, and save Evans' life.

Tom Crean came to the Antarctic once more, in 1914, with Ernest Shackleton. Shackleton planned to cross the whole continent but the expedition was a disaster. (Read the entry under Shackleton to find out why.) Tom Crean was one of the men who sailed in the little *James Caird* on the incredible journey for help. 'He always sang while he was steering, and nobody ever discovered what the song was,' said Shackleton. 'Yet somehow it was cheerful.' Crean went with Shackleton on the final terrible climb over the mountains.

After all his adventures Tom Crean went home to Ireland and settled down to run the South Pole Inn.

CREVASSE

Crevasses are the stuff of nightmares. 'I still dream about them,' wrote one of the men on Scott's expedition long afterwards. 'I loathe them. You never knew when you would be dropping into some bottomless pit, or rushing to help some companion who had disappeared. Coming back down the Beardmore Glacier a man on our sledge went down head first, another fell in eight times in twenty-five minutes. He looked pretty dazed. Always as you fell you wondered if your harness would hold, and you waited for the sudden jerk.'

Crevasses are deep cracks in the ice with blue-green icy sides. Stresses in the ice cause it to split. The ice might be flowing over hidden rocks, or moving fast downhill. The ice twists, and stretches, and breaks apart. Crevasses can form in several directions crisscrossing through the ice. They are anything from a few centimetres to thirty metres wide, and usually thirty to forty metres deep. The sailors on Scott's expedition saw crevasses in the Beardmore Glacier wide enough to swallow their ship, twice over.

Crevasses are often hidden. Snow bridges cover their tops and the surface looks safe. The danger lurks beneath. The snow bridge might be strong enough to take a man's weight. Or it might not.

A SKIDOO CROSSING A CREVASSE

Tuesday 21 February 1911, Scott's expedition.

Dogs were pulling a sledge across the ice. Suddenly they disappeared like rats down a hole. The sledge was left on one side of a crevasse, with the last two dogs. The powerful lead dog clung to the snow on the other. Dangling in the middle in a festoon were ten howling frightened dogs, scrabbling against the sides of the ice. Two fell out of their harness on to a ledge twenty metres down in the great blue chasm. Two fought every time they swung near enough to bite each other. The weight of the dogs in the crevasse was dragging the lead dog towards the edge. Men rushed to unload the sledge and save the lead dog. One man went down by rope into the crevasse and began cutting the dogs loose and hauling them out. It was cold work. After an hour and a half eight dogs were up on the ice. Then Scott was lowered down into the crevasse on a rope to save the two dogs on the ledge. While he was down there the rescued dogs began a furious fight with the dogs in the second sledge team, barking, biting, even though some were injured.

DESERT

The Antarctic has most of the world's fresh water. But the water is trapped as ice.

Antarctica is so cold almost all water falls on it as snow. Over much of the interior less than five centimetres of snow falls a year. The average for the whole continent is only twelve to fifteen centimetres a year. This makes Antarctica the driest continent and one of the most arid deserts on Earth.

DOGS

Compare a husky dog with a human in the Antarctic. Dogs don't need a tent, sleeping bag, or clothes. They curl up tight and sleep in the snow. Their thick hair protects them from blizzards. The Antarctic, said the Norwegian explorer Amundsen, is made for dogs.

Amundsen used teams of dogs to pull his loaded sledges to the South Pole and back. He knew that dogs could work in the snow and ice because he had used them in the Arctic. Amundsen wasn't romantic about dogs. They had to learn to obey and respect their master. They sometimes fought each other to the death. They ate each other if they were hungry. Amundsen also knew that dogs gave important companionship to lonely men. He knew that dogs needed looking after as carefully as humans.

Early British explorers were less sure about dogs. They didn't understand how to get dogs to pull sledges. They wanted dogs to be their companions yet despised the way they fought and scavenged.

Strong broad-chested husky dogs had been used to haul loads in far northern countries for centuries. Many explorers bought dogs in Greenland, northern America, or Russia, and carried them on the long sea journey to Antarctica. They packed dried fish, meat, and biscuit to feed to the dogs. But the dogs thrived on fresh seal. Lost or abandoned dogs survived for weeks by killing seals.

A properly trained well-fed dog team moved fast and efficiently over the snow. When Lieutenant Evans lay dying out on the ice in February 1912, a dog team was sent to rescue him. 'We heard the baying of the dogs,' said Evans. 'They galloped right up to the tent door, and the leader, a beautiful grey dog . . . came right into the tent and licked my hands and face. I put my poor weak hands up and gripped his furry ears . . . I kissed his old, hairy face.' In three hours the dogs carried Evans to safety. A man had taken eighteen hours to walk that distance.

Once machines came to the Antarctic, dogs were used less often. But a few dog teams are still used, although some people object that seals must be killed to feed them. Specially trained huskies were flown in from America by the Trans-Antarctic Expedition in 1989 to pull their sledges across the continent.

DRYGALSKI

Professor Erich von Drygalski planned to spend the winter in Antarctica. But the pack ice trapped his ship *Gauss*, which had left Germany in August 1901. In the distance Drygalski could see ice cliffs which he was sure formed part of the Antarctic continent. His men sledged to the ice cliffs and named the land Kaiser Wilhelm II Land after the German Emperor.

Drygalski's official German expedition included well-qualified scientists. *Gauss* was specially built and comfortable, lit with electricity generated by a windmill. Much scientific work was done. Even the sounds made by penguins were recorded. But Drygalski was disappointed to reach only the edge of Antarctica.

DRY VALLEYS

Very very little of Antarctica is free of snow and ice. A few cliffs and headlands rise from the sea, there are some pebbly beaches, and rocky mountains. But there are also mysterious valleys and hills of bare brown, black and yellow rock. This is Antarctica 'with the skin peeled back', the shape of the continent without its white covering. The most famous of these 'oases' are the Dry Valleys in Victoria Land.

No rain has fallen in the Dry Valleys for two million years. Nothing grows. Nothing moves. The wind blows, eating away at the rocks. These cold barren valleys and hills are the driest places on Earth. They are the nearest thing we have to the landscapes of the Moon or Mars. The only living things are microbes and little groups of fungi, algae, and lichen which survive inside rocks.

The glaciers which once ground down these valleys were pushed back when the shape of the land changed and new mountains rose up. Now the warmth of the sun in summer melts winter snow. The wind dries out the moisture, and snow and ice do not accumulate.

Scientists study the Dry Valleys, but it is impossible to avoid polluting them. Nothing decays in the dry cold. Every footstep disturbs the surface which only the wind has touched for hundreds of thousands of years. Camping scientists bring everything they need in with them, and they try to take everything out.

DUMONT D'URVILLE

For five Antarctic summers, 1838–43, ships from the French, British, and American navies explored in Antarctic seas. All hoped to discover land, and the South Magnetic Pole. The United States sent six ships led by Charles Wilkes. James Clark Ross commanded two British ships. Captain Dumont d'Urville of France commanded *Astrolabe* and *Zelée*. D'Urville had already sailed twice around the world, exploring and collecting scientific specimens.

The French saw islands at the tip of the Antarctic Peninsula in February 1838. But their great discovery came a year later in January 1839 when high snow-covered land appeared, stretching as far as they could see. They sailed towards the land between huge sparkling icebergs – as if we were in the narrow streets of a city of giants, said d'Urville – and found a tiny rocky island where it was possible to beach their boats. Shoving aside the penguins, they raised the flag, drank a bottle of wine and claimed the new land for France. Then they searched for something to take home. There were no shells, or plants, not even a scrap of lichen. So they knocked a few flakes off the rocks, shouted 'hurrah' in the great silence, and rowed back to their ships.

Dumont d'Urville was missing his wife, Adélie, and named the land after her. The penguins were given her name as well.

▲ Pancake ice – discs of thin sea ice
which form on the water's surface

▲ Wandering albatross in flight

◀ Adélie penguins making their way across sea ice

▼ Emperor penguins, one with a young chick

▲ Husky dog

▲ The 6cm krill. An estimated
six thousand million million
live in the sea around
Antarctica

▲ A Weddell seal with her new-born pup
Another with a four-week old baby ▼

▲ Crabeater seals swimming under a tide crack in the ice

◄ Leopard seal lying on an ice floe

▼ A killer whale lifts its head out of the water checking for prey

▲ Scott, standing (centre) at
the South Pole, with Oates
(left) and Evans (right).
Bowers (left) and Wilson
(right) are sitting

◀ Tabular iceberg

▼ An aerial view of part of the
Transverse Mountains on the
Antarctic Peninsula

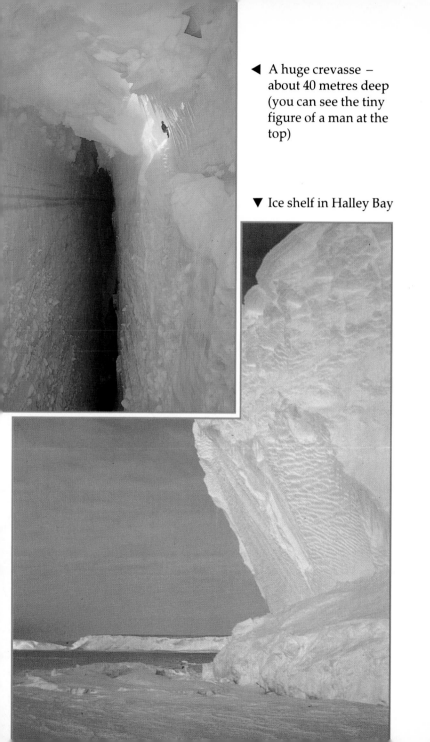

◀ A huge crevasse – about 40 metres deep (you can see the tiny figure of a man at the top)

▼ Ice shelf in Halley Bay

▲ A team of huskies pulling a wooden sledge

◀ Skidoos and sledges

▼ South Pole surrounded by flags of Antarctic Treaty countries

ELEPHANT SEALS

Sometimes a young male elephant seal comes on shore in Antarctica. His bulk makes him different from all other seals. But if he goes on to become a beachmaster in charge of thirty to a hundred females he will be a huge seal, covered in scars from fighting other males. The successful bull weighs four tonnes, and is four to seven times heavier than the female. He can inflate his nose and roar through it. His breath is disgusting.

No one knows much about where elephant seals go when they are not on their breeding beaches in the islands and along the Antarctic Peninsula. But every year they come back to the same beaches, which heave with smelly, noisy, enormous, blubbery bodies. Vast numbers of elephant seals were killed for their oil. Now sealing has stopped, and there are probably three-quarters of a million elephant seals.

EMPEROR PENGUINS

In the desperate cold and darkness of winter, an animal stands on the Antarctic ice. He is tall, over a metre high, and his chest is nearly as broad as a man's. His only protection against the howling gales and freezing blizzards is tough waterproof feathers and a layer of fat. He ate his last meal two months ago. But he must stay here standing on the ice.

Balanced on his horny feet is an egg.

Week after week, standing tall in the gloom, getting thinner and thinner, the male Emperor penguin looks after the egg. A special fold of skin keeps the egg warm. When the bitter blizzards blow he shuffles slowly towards the other males and they huddle together, backs to the wind. Ten Emperors can pack tightly into a square metre. The ones at the back get so cold they shuffle slowly, egg on feet, around the huddle to the front, away from the wind. As more penguins peel away and move to the front the huddle gradually moves across the ice, and each penguin finds himself in the centre before once again being at the back. So every penguin gets a turn at being warm.

For nine weeks and two days he tries to keep the egg off the ice, warm and safe. When the chick hatches he reaches down to the little creature standing on his feet, under the fold of skin, and feeds it with a milky mixture from inside his gullet.

Over the ice, in the darkness, travelling enormous distances in from the sea where they have been feeding, the females come back to find their mates. As soon as they laid their eggs they left for the sea. Now, somewhere in the crowds and darkness each must find her partner. Each pair has a special song. Calling, calling, among the thousands of birds, they find each other. Sometimes the female comes in time to hatch the egg herself. Sometimes she is too late. Her mate, exhausted and starving, has abandoned the egg to save his own life.

The thin, dirty, weary males set off for the sea. They have eaten nothing for one hundred and fifteen days. They have lost nearly half their weight. Now they must travel between eighty and three hundred kilometres across the ice to the water, and food.

At first the chick sits on its mother's feet, eating food regurgitated from her stomach, and learning to recognize her special call. She bends forward and sings loudly while the chick whistles and bobs its little head. The chick stands on the ice with the other chicks when it gets too big to fit on its parents' feet. Chicks have only five months to grow large enough to look after themselves. A lot of chicks fail. The parents work hard collecting food. But the journey to and from the open sea across the winter ice takes so long. The chicks get occasional massive meals, then nothing.

When they are only just big enough the chicks begin their own journey across the ice. They have to find the sea and start feeding while it is still summer. Some years not many survive from egg to the ocean. Other years perhaps two out of three manage. But if they do become adults, Emperor penguins can live to be fifty.

Emperors are the world's biggest penguins. They dive deeper than any other birds in their search for food. An Emperor's dive has been measured at four hundred and fifty-eight metres, and they may go deeper. They breed in the most extreme conditions faced by any bird or animal. Early explorers were impressed by the grave, stately manner of these beautiful birds. But when they discovered the penguins actually lived on the continent through the dreadful Antarctic winter, they were appalled. 'I do not believe anybody on earth has a worse time than an Emperor penguin,' said one of the first men to study them.

EMPEROR PENGUINS HUDDLING IN WINTER

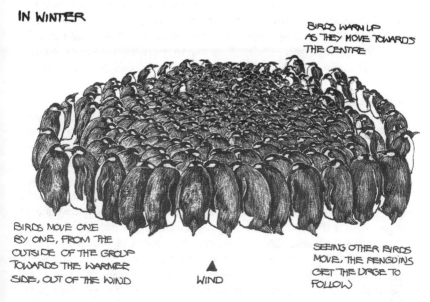

BIRDS WARM UP AS THEY MOVE TOWARDS THE CENTRE

BIRDS MOVE ONE BY ONE, FROM THE OUTSIDE OF THE GROUP TOWARDS THE WARMER SIDE, OUT OF THE WIND

WIND

SEEING OTHER BIRDS MOVE, THE PENGUINS GET THE URGE TO FOLLOW

EMPERORS' EGGS

Their clothes were frozen stiff like suits of armour. Their sleeping bags were frozen into hard boxes. Every morning they stuffed clothes into the tops so the bags froze open. Then every night they could push their legs into the frozen holes and start the long painful horrible business of getting their bodies in. But their bodies wouldn't stop shaking with the cold. After a couple of hours the bags warmed, and the ice began to thaw. One morning Cherry came out of the tent. As he lifted his head his clothes froze. For the next four hours he pulled the sledge with his head stuck back unable to move it. After that everyone came out of the tent bent into the sledge-pulling position so their clothes froze the right way.

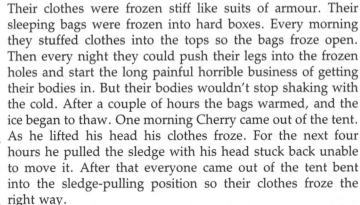

Night and morning meant nothing anyway. It was all the same in the winter darkness. They couldn't see to put up the tent, or where they were going. They blundered on across the ice dragging the two heavily loaded sledges. Their breath froze in sheets down their faces. Their hats were frozen like metal caps to their heads. They were desperately cold and tired. They were the first people to try travelling in an Antarctic winter. And they were suffering all this to collect some eggs from the Emperor penguin, to take back to scientists in London.

After nineteen days they got near the place where the penguins were. They built a hut of rocks with a roof of canvas. Then they struggled over crevasses and ice cliffs, collected five precious eggs, groped their way back in the darkness, with two eggs broken, and collapsed exhausted into the hut.

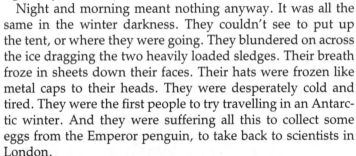

A blizzard began. The canvas roof crashed up and down with a frightful, deafening noise. Their tent pitched just outside blew away. After twenty-four hours the canvas roof split into shreds with a noise like gunfire and rocks from the walls fell in on them. 'Roll over!' someone shouted. 'Lie on your stomachs.' The snow piled in and the wind blew with great violence. 'I paddled my feet inside my bag and sang all the songs and hymns I knew to pass the time,' said Birdie

Bowers. 'Occasionally I thumped Bill, and as he still moved I knew he was alive. It was his thirty-ninth birthday. What a birthday! 'I tried to join in singing, a bit feebly,' said Cherry. 'We had been in the freezing cold and dark for four weeks. Everything we had was sopping. What chance did we have? Without the tent we were dead men.' Every now and then they opened the flaps of their sleeping bags and put little pinches of snow in their mouths.

After two days and nights they managed to have a meal. The blizzard slowed. And then, miraculously, they found the tent, blown down an icy slope, but usable. 'Our lives,' said Cherry-Garrard, 'had been taken away and given back to us.'

The three men survived. When they got back to their base at Cape Evans seven days later, on 1 August 1911, they were exhausted, frost-bitten, thin. 'Their looks haunted me for days,' said one of their companions. Two of the men, Edward Wilson and twenty-eight-year-old Birdie Bowers, died with Scott eight months later. The twenty-five-year-old Apsley Cherry-Garrard survived, to take the penguin eggs back to the Natural History Museum in London.

ESKIMOS

The first men to live on the Antarctic Continent came back to civilization in 1900 and sent a message to their friends in Europe that they were safe. Along the telegraph lines from Europe came the first question: 'Did you find any people down there?'

Antarctica was as mysterious as the Moon. No one even knew its shape. Only small pieces of coast had ever been seen. Why shouldn't there be people living in the south? Eskimos lived in the north Polar regions.

But no humans were living in Antarctica. None had ever lived there. No people were attacked, no ancient civilizations damaged, by the first humans to come. This tenth of the world's land surface was empty of people, and always had been.

Humans are only visitors to Antarctica.

FACE MASKS

Working out ways of protecting the face against extreme cold produced some wonderful inventions. Birdie Bowers in 1911 made a hat he was very proud of. It was complicated, with nose guards, strings, and buttons. But when he wore the hat his breath froze it solid like an iron helmet, and he could not look down without moving his whole body. He had to be chipped out of it.

Richard Byrd wore a mask made of wire with windproof cloth over it. He breathed up a funnel which led to the nose, and out of another funnel which led to the mouth. It quickly clogged with ice which had to be brushed out.

FANCY DRESS BALL

A fancy dress ball was held on an ice floe on New Year's Eve 1841. Captain James Clark Ross's ship *Erebus* was tied up on one side of the floe. Commander Francis Crozier's ship *Terror* was tied up on the other side. The ballroom was carved into the ice and decorated with ice statues. A well-stocked 'Antarctic Hotel' had bar and seats made of ice. Ice thrones were carved for the two ships' captains. There was music, dancing and games. At midnight everyone made as much noise as they could. Sailors carried the ships' pigs under their arms like bagpipes, and squeezed them till they squealed. Then there was a huge snowball fight.

The two ships and the ice floe drifted on quietly across the Antarctic Circle, and warm Polar clothing was handed out to all the men.

FEET

Feet get cold faster than any other part of the body and they stay cold longer. The best way of keeping feet warm in snow is to wear boots that are too big. This helps the blood to circulate around the feet. But the real problem is moisture which freezes inside boots forming a layer of ice.

Early explorers wore soft boots made of reindeer skin called

MODERN FLEXIBLE BOOT

MUKLUK

FINNESKOE

finnesko. They lined their socks with a special grass which grew in northern Norway called 'sennegrass'. At the end of a day the frozen sweat shook out of the grass.

Men quickly learned to take care of their feet. Brush the snow off boots before coming into the tent. Don't leave wet socks on. Keep drying socks, somehow. Don't take boots off and leave them lying out of shape or they freeze crooked and feet have to be forced in next morning.

Knowing if a foot had frozen wasn't easy. It was important to keep checking whether there was any feeling left. If it did freeze, there was only one cure. The frozen foot had to be put against the warmth of someone's skin. A friend would pull open his shirt, and lay the foot against his stomach. Slowly the circulation would come back, and with it excruciating pounding pain.

Today people wear flexible boots with socks and quilted boot-liners. The boots have thick soles and springy inners to insulate the foot from snow or ice.

FIRE

In the land of ice and cold one of the greatest dangers is fire. Fires burn fiercely in the dry air. Doors to the outside are often blocked with drift snow. People risk losing everything which protects them and keeps them alive because there are no spares around the corner in Antarctica. Many bases are built with emergency supplies separate from the main building, or with living, sleeping, and working areas in different buildings.

There is no water to put out the flames. The water is all trapped as ice.

FIRST MOTORS

The first – and only – motor car on the Antarctic continent came with Shackleton in 1907. The driver of the Arrol-Johnston sat in the open on a leather seat. Shackleton hoped the car would pull heavy loads over the ice, but it bogged in the soft snow and had to be abandoned.

Scott brought three motorized sledges which ran on caterpillar tracks to the Antarctic in 1911. They were extremely expensive. A motor sledge cost the same as six hundred and sixty husky dogs. They had no steering or brakes, and could travel at about 3-4 kph. Scott wanted the sledges to carry loads across the ice. But they had to carry their own petrol, oil, spare parts, tool kit, and driver before anything else could be added.

One motor sledge broke through the ice and sank as it was being unloaded from the ship. The other two travelled just over a week towards the Pole before they broke down and had to be abandoned. Snow quickly covered them, and they began to slide slowly towards the sea.

FISH

The first scientists working in Antarctica tried hard to catch fish. They wanted to look at the kind of fish which could survive such cold water. Their friends also wanted to catch fish – to eat.

People have gone on wanting to eat Antarctic fish, and already some areas have been over-fished. Scientists have found out that Antarctic fish grow slowly, mature slowly, and produce few eggs. So they do not replace themselves very fast, and are very vulnerable.

Salt water freezes at about −1.9°C. Sea water in Antarctica is nearly always below 0°C. Normal fishes' blood would freeze at this temperature. But most Antarctic fish have antifreeze in their body fluids. One kind of fish, the ghostly-looking icefish, has white blood with no red blood corpuscles, and no scales. Most of Antarctica's two hundred species of fish belong to families that are not found anywhere else.

FLEAS

Antarctic fleas include one of the largest fleas in the world – up to six millimetres long. Home to these giant fleas is a sea bird, usually a petrel. They live deep in the feathers, protected from cold water and icy winds by the oil which waterproofs the bird and keeps it dry. A thousand Antarctic fleas can live on one bird getting all the shelter, warmth, and food they need.

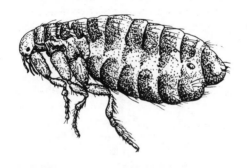

FOOD

Half-eaten bread rolls lay on the table, with bottles of pickles and sauces. Crisp gingerbread biscuits were piled in a tin. But the men who walked away from this meal had left years before. Now some of them were back in Antarctica. They opened the door of the hut – and there was the food exactly as they had left it. The gingerbread tasted as good as ever.

Antarctica is a giant freezer. Everything is preserved. Food brought south eighty years ago could be eaten today.

Enormous amounts of food came on the early expeditions. Men wanted to eat familiar things so far from home. The British sat down to fresh bread and jam, the Norwegians to steaming hot cakes. The British celebrated with roast beef and Yorkshire pudding, the Australians with roast mutton. At base camp men ate well, especially if the cook was good. 'Treats' were saved up for

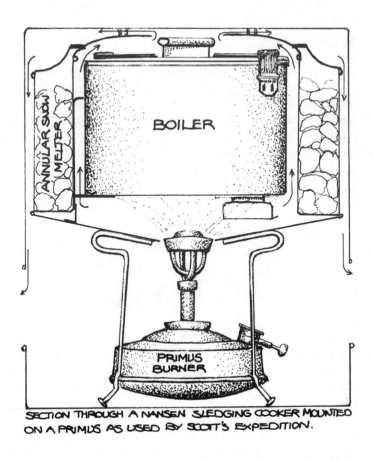

SECTION THROUGH A NANSEN SLEDGING COOKER MOUNTED ON A PRIMUS AS USED BY SCOTT'S EXPEDITION.

special occasions. Amundsen's cook slept with bottles of champagne secretly in his bed to stop them freezing. When the Norwegians returned from the South Pole in triumph, the champagne was ready.

On expeditions away from base, food was a real problem. Everything had to be carried, cooked quickly and eaten under difficult conditions. Sledging was hard work and men had huge appetites. All expedition leaders worried about what food to take and how much. Everyone agreed on simple sledging rations. The basic food was 'pemmican' – dried meat mixed with fat – and large baked biscuits. Each biscuit was made specially thick and hard so it wouldn't break.

'They were like rocks,' said Mawson. 'We smashed them with an ice-axe, or soaked fragments in cocoa.'

Amundsen added oatmeal and dried peas to his pemmican, and took only chocolate and dried milk as extras on his Polar journey. Scott took cocoa, butter, sugar, and tea as extras. All of the sledging rations lacked vital ingredients for healthy living.

Today expeditioners eat vitamin and mineral supplements to make up for lack of fresh food. Sledging rations include freeze-dried vegetables, soups and milk, and muesli bars, jam, and oatmeal. The six men on the Trans-Antarctic Expedition (1989–90) ate oatmeal and butter for breakfast, dried fruit, nuts, chocolate, and muesli bars for lunch, and pemmican, peanut butter, soup, cheese, and a choice of noodles, rice, or potatoes for dinner – one thousand and twenty grammes of food each per day, five thousand calories.

FOOD DREAMS

Really hungry men dreamed about food. They dreamed of sticky buns and chocolate, afternoon tea under the trees with rich fruit cake, big dinners in the City with roast beef. Most men woke up before they managed to eat anything. They sat down at a banquet and the food was whisked away. They went around the corner to a shop and it was closed. They bought a delicious cake at a stall and woke up just as it reached their lips. But some lucky men ate their dream meals. Everyone was jealous when they described the food in the morning. After all, a dream meal was better than nothing.

FOOD – FAIR DIVISIONS

This is how hungry men shared their food. One man in a group divided the food into as near equal portions as he could. One of the others turned his back on the food and closed his eyes. The first man pointed to a portion. 'Whose is this?' The man with his back turned called out a name. 'And whose is this?' He called out another name, until all the food was handed out.

What you got might be a mixture of crumbled old biscuit, seal meat, hairs from the sleeping bags, and pieces of grit, but it was the same as everyone else's. And it was food.

FOSSILS

Fossils are evidence about the past, proof of what once was. It isn't easy to find fossils in Antarctica because most rock is hidden under ice. But fossils of plants and animals have been discovered proving that Antarctica has had warm climates. Large animals roamed amongst thickly growing plants. Many creatures lived in shallow seas. Some of the fossils match those found in other southern continents, which helps prove that Antarctica was the keystone of the large southern supercontinent, Gondwana. About twenty-eight million years ago Antarctica became completely surrounded by ocean. The climate grew steadily colder and colder killing plants and animals.

FROST-BITE

It is easy to be frost-bitten on the face without knowing. The cold freezes a patch of skin on the nose or cheek. If the skin is massaged straight away the blood flows back, really hurting. People watched each other for the tell-tale patches of dead-white skin and gave the warning.

Frost-bitten toes and fingers are white, cold and numb. They must be warmed fast. If the tissue dies, gangrene can set in and the injured part must be amputated.

FUCHS

Ernest Shackleton wanted to be first across the Antarctic continent. His party was trapped in pack ice in 1915 and didn't even land. British explorer Vivian Fuchs planned the first overland journey across the continent using the same general scheme as Shackleton. But as well as dogs and sledges he used the latest technology. The Commonwealth Trans-Antarctic Expedition began in 1955 with ships able to push through pack ice, and aircraft to find routes ahead and carry supplies. Fuchs could keep all parts of his expedition in touch by radio. He used Sno-Cats and tractors. The Americans had just established their base at the South Pole, so there were people in the middle of the journey. Even then two difficult dangerous years were spent in Antarctica building bases, laying depots and surveying routes before the crossing could begin.

The three thousand four hundred and seventy-two kilometre journey took ninety-nine days from 24 November 1957 to 2 March 1958, Weddell Sea to Ross Sea. Each vehicle dragged one or two sledges. Lurching slowly across the huge icy distances in often appalling conditions they broke down, sank into crevasses, were hauled out, repaired, maintained, abandoned. Three Sno-Cats survived the crossing led by Fuchs's big orange 'Rock 'n' Roll'.

FUTURE OF ANTARCTICA

Will humans take what they can from Antarctica? Will hungry people fish the food they need from the Southern Ocean, mine the metals they want from the rock, drill for oil and gas hidden under the ice? Will nations keep pieces of Antarctica for themselves? Or will humans decide to treat this huge icy continent differently from the way they have treated the rest of our planet? We have made many mistakes in the past. Can we manage not to repeat them?

At least we are lucky to have discovered Antarctica so recently. We have new understanding of the way our planet works, how every living thing depends on everything else.

Our planet is four thousand six hundred and fifty million years old. During only the last million years the great ice sheets of Antarctica have melted and re-formed, oceans have risen and receded, there have been droughts and floods. Antarctica has changed in the past and it will change in the future. We do not understand what causes these mighty changes. But we do know that our actions as humans are now affecting Antarctica. We cannot afford wrong decisions.

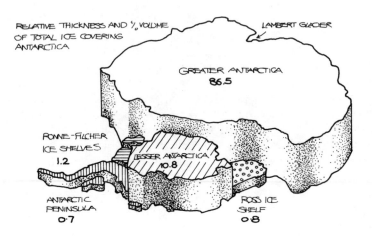

RELATIVE THICKNESS AND % VOLUME OF TOTAL ICE COVERING ANTARCTICA

LAMBERT GLACIER

GREATER ANTARCTICA
86.5

RONNE-FILCHNER ICE SHELVES
1.2

LESSER ANTARCTICA
10.8

ANTARCTIC PENINSULA
0.7

ROSS ICE SHELF
0.8

GLACIERS

Enormous glaciers pour from Antarctica's high ice sheet towards the coast. They force through the mountains, their surfaces cracked and seamed with crevasses and spectacular ice falls. The glaciers feed into the ice shelves or end directly in the sea.

The world's largest valley glacier is in Antarctica. The Lambert Glacier flows four hundred kilometres into an ice shelf. When it reaches the sea three hundred kilometres further on, it is two hundred kilometres wide.

GLOBAL POLLUTION

Locked up in the Antarctic ice is the history of Earth's atmosphere and climates. Antarctica's ice sheet is the cleanest area in the world. Yet it is full of tiny impurities. As snow crystals form and fall they 'scavenge' particles out of the air. Ash from volcanoes, radioactive dust, insecticides, dust from dry deserts, pollen, lead, all are trapped by Antarctica's snow as it falls, layer upon layer, year after year. Minute bubbles of air are trapped as well. Slowly the snow is squeezed and turns into ice. The particles and air bubbles are frozen into the ice sheet, locked in permanently.

Scientists drill down and bring up cores of ice from deep inside the ice sheet. Each core is a precious slice of the world's past. The ice is laid down in layers a bit like tree rings. Scientists date the layers, and study samples of ice to piece together vital clues about Earth's history. But all clothing and equipment must be ultra clean to avoid contaminating these precious samples.

Here in Antarctica's ice is evidence about pollution, natural and man-made, and the kinds of climate Earth used to have. Here is evidence for the way things were, and are now. So far scientists have tracked back through one hundred and fifty thousand years of our planet's history.

Antarctica's ice gives us a way of measuring increases in pollutants. It is one of the best methods we have for seeing what humans are doing to the world environment. We now for example have proof that the greenhouse gas carbon dioxide has increased by ten per cent in the last thirty years.

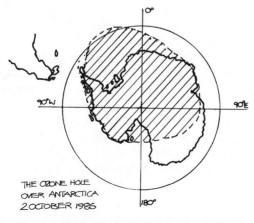

THE OZONE HOLE
OVER ANTARCTICA
2 OCTOBER 1986

GLOBAL WARMING

If world air temperatures rose, the effect on Antarctica could be devastating. The ice shelves could break up. The pack ice might not form.

One part of Antarctica's ice is especially vulnerable – the West Antarctic Ice Sheet. It rests on bedrock which is below sea level. If it melted completely the seas would rise around the world by five metres.

Even a rise of one metre would cause chaos in many countries. Some scientists predict this could happen once the greenhouse effect really begins.

But no one knows what will happen. Measuring the stability of Antarctica's ice, finding out whether the same amount of pack ice forms every year, whether the continent loses more ice than it gains, is vital. What happens in Antarctica can give early warning of global changes. Antarctica's ice is of vital concern to us all.

GLOBAL WEATHER

Not much sunlight falls on Antarctica. What does is mostly shot back up into space. The sun reflects off the white snow and ice and radiates back without being turned into heat.

Antarctica is a giant cooling system for the planet. Every year the region loses more heat than it gains. But most of the world's heat loss takes place in Antarctica's winter, when huge amounts of sea ice cover the Southern Ocean, and the ice-covered area of Antarctica is nearly one-tenth of the planet's surface.

Air moves around Earth's atmosphere largely because of the difference in temperature between the warm tropics and the cold Poles. The largest difference is in the south so the greatest air movements happen here. Antarctica is extremely important to global weather.

If Antarctica's ice increased, temperatures could drop even further, causing more ice, and more heat loss. If Antarctica's ice lessened, the air temperatures could rise, melting more ice. Both these things have happened during the last million years of our planet's history. Some scientists think Antarctica is the key to changes in global climate.

Meteorologists have been studying Antarctica's weather from the first expeditions. Men struggled outside at four-hourly intervals to read maximum and minimum temperatures, and wind speed and direction. They tried launching balloons to gather information from high in the atmosphere. Now many measurements are done automatically by unmanned stations and satellites. Twenty-five manned meteorological stations operate year round on the continent. Scientists work to understand Antarctica's crucial role in global weather patterns.

GLOVES

Put your glove down in the Antarctic and the wind blows it away. Lose a glove and your hand gets frost-bitten. Explorers sewed their gloves on to cords and attached them to a 'harness' which they wore over their jackets.

Men wore fingerless mittens because fingers stay warmer when they touch each other. Over the top they wore more mittens – of felt, wool or lambskin. For very cold weather they had long mitts made of wolfskin, ponyskin, or bearskin.

GOGGLES

Goggles or tinted glasses must be worn in Antarctica to protect the eyes against snow blindness, which is caused by the glare of reflected sunlight off snow and ice.

Snow blindness is terribly painful. Men attacked by snow blindness bandaged their eyes to escape from the light. They stumbled along, tied to a sledge, unable to see.

Goggles and glasses easily mist up with sweat, which freezes. The Eskimos had goggles made of wood or bone with little slits to keep out most of the light. Amundsen used goggles based on the Eskimo model, with ventilation slits on the top.

GONDWANA

Antarctica was once the centre of an enormous supercontinent which scientists call 'Gondwana'. One hundred and eighty million years ago Gondwana began to break up. What is now Africa and India split up and drifted away. By fifty-five million years ago the southern coast of Australia had separated from Antarctica and Australia started drifting north. The Antarctic Peninsula divided from the tip of South America about twenty-eight million years ago. Antarctica was now alone, surrounded by ocean. A strong current flowed around the continent separating it from warmer oceans to the north. Antarctica began to get colder.

GREENPEACE

Greenpeace set up a small year-round scientific station in Antarctica in 1987 on Ross Island, near Scott's old hut at Cape Evans. Four or five people spend the winter working at the base – a leader, a radio technician, a medical officer, and one or two scientists.

Greenpeace believes it is important to have a base in Antarctica which does not represent a particular government, since they fear that competition for Antarctica's resources will hurt the continent. They want a permanent ban on mining in Antarctica. They believe Antarctica should be preserved now, and for the future, by declaring it a World Park.

Greenpeace studies the way humans have affected Antarctica. Many bases have large rubbish dumps. The seabed off the American base at McMurdo Sound is contaminated and polluted. Fuel containers, broken machinery, plastic, old batteries, pile up outside some stations against the agreements of the Antarctic Treaty. For years people have thrown aside what they don't want. But nothing decomposes in the dry air. Greenpeace helps persuade governments to deal with their mess.

GROWLERS

Growlers are pieces of green ice, 'treacherous fragments' as Shackleton called them, which float almost under water. They are very dangerous to small ships.

HALLEY STATION

A line of oil drums across the ice marks the safe route to Halley Station from the sea. All you find when you get there are radio masts and large boxes which hide the shafts to the underground buildings. One has a London Underground sign. A signpost gives distances: one thousand six hundred and six kilometres to the South Pole, two thousand eight hundred and thirty-four kilometres to the American base at McMurdo, fourteen thousand two hundred and seventy-five kilometres to London, four hundred and thirty-eight kilometres to the nearest humans at the Argentinian base General Belgrano.

Each of the four previous British bases built here on the Brunt Ice Shelf has been crushed by snow and ice. According to measurements made by satellite, this, the fifth base since 1956, is being carried along in the ice seven hundred and fifty metres a year.

Scientists study the upper atmosphere, especially aurorae, the ionosphere, radio waves, and ozone. Research done here at Halley first revealed the drastic thinning of the ozone layer.

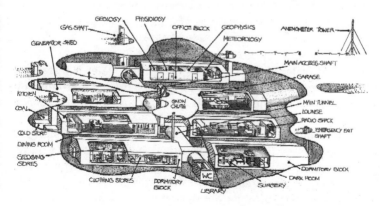

HILLARY

New Zealander Sir Edmund Hillary was one of the two men who first climbed Mount Everest. Four years later in 1957 he went to Antarctica as part of the Commonwealth Trans-Antarctic Expedition. Hillary led the first party to travel overland to the South Pole since Scott in 1912. He arrived in the first vehicles to drive to the Pole – three farm tractors fitted with rubber treads.

At the Pole he joined Fuchs who had already travelled from the other side of Antarctica. Fuchs finished the first crossing of the continent using the route and supplies organized by the New Zealanders.

HOOSH

Hoosh is the hot meal that used to be eaten on a sledging journey.

'Hoosh,' wrote Douglas Mawson, 'is a stodgy, porridge-like mixture of pemmican, dried biscuit, and water, brought to the boil and served hot. Some men prefer it cooler and more dilute, and . . . dig up snow from the floor of the tent with their spoons, and mix it in . . . Eating hoosh is a heightened form of bliss which no sledger can ever forget.'

Different hooshes were made by adding new ingredients – like seal, horse, curry powder, sugar, oatmeal, or chocolate – to the mixture.

ICE

Ice is frozen water. Most of the world's fresh water is in fact ice. Ninety-nine per cent of our planet's surface fresh water is held as snow, ice, glaciers, and ice sheets. About nine-tenths of this is in Antarctica.

The snow falling on Antarctica packs down. New snow squeezes the layers of snow underneath pushing the crystals more tightly together. As more snow falls, increasing the pressure, the crystals of snow change size and shape. Gradually all the air spaces are closed off and the snow becomes glacier ice, clear and hard, the ice of most of Antarctica's ice sheet. The number of years this takes, and the depth at which it happens, varies. On an ice shelf near the coast, glacier ice forms quite fast in two to three hundred years, about thirty-six to sixty metres below the surface.

Ice seems rock hard. Unmoving. In fact ice is unstable, shifting stuff. It gives like elastic. It flows under its own weight. It slides like treacle or wet cement. It bends and twists and sinks and slips and cracks open. It squeaks and groans and roars.

Antarctica is ice. It has endured an ice age for millions of years.

ICEBERGS

Icebergs are great floating islands of the snow that once fell on Antarctica. The layers of snow packed down and turned into ice. Over thousands of years the ice slides towards the edges of the continent where it breaks off in great slabs and falls into the sea. Huge flat-topped pieces 'calve' from the ice shelves. Some icebergs tumble from glaciers with a thunderous roar. Thousands and thousands of icebergs float in the ocean around Antarctica. One million three hundred thousand cubic kilometres of ice break away from the continent into the sea every year. The icebergs drift around Antarctica at about five hundred metres an hour. The largest can be tracked by satellite. Some icebergs get trapped near the shore when they run aground on the sea floor.

Slowly the sea works into weak places in the ice, making great

USUALLY ABOUT 4/5 OF AN ICEBERG ARE SUBMERGED

caves. Waves rush in and out with a hollow roar. Air trapped in the ice for thousands of years fizzes out. The icebergs glow a magnificent blue, with emerald green shadows, or dazzle with the whitest white. Huge bergs break up into smaller pieces, eroding and melting into beautiful fantastic shapes. As an iceberg rots and ages it can suddenly roll over. The water boils and seethes as the colossal lump of ice heaves up, water streaming from its sides, and floats upside down. Gradually the bergs drift north into warmer seas, melting away to nothing. Most are finished by the time they reach the Antarctic Convergence, after a life of four to six years.

Antarctica's icebergs are unique. In the Arctic icebergs are fewer and smaller. There are none of Antarctica's great 'tabular' bergs which can be well over a hundred kilometres long. Antarctic bergs have more air bubbles than Arctic bergs, so float higher in the water. Even then four-fifths of an Antarctic iceberg is below sea level.

Could icebergs give their water to dry countries? Icebergs are huge quarries of the purest water in the world. All this fresh water melts into the sea, playing a very important part in the way the Southern Ocean works. People have tried to think out methods of towing icebergs north, but there are many difficulties. Icebergs must be chosen with no hidden faults. Half an iceberg's bulk would melt on the journey. It would stick on the sea floor a long way off shore. One idea is to surround an iceberg with a plastic sheet. Fresh water melting off the berg would form a reservoir which could be pumped out.

ICE-BREAKER

Ice-breakers push through the kind of pack ice which traps other ships. But if the ice is particularly thick the Captain can use specially powerful turbine engines. Tremendous power is built up. The ship backs off from the ice. Then it advances, and rams. The bow rises up onto the ice. The propellers thunder. The ship shudders. Slowly a crack opens across the ice as the weight of the ship breaks it. The ship lurches off into the black water and huge chunks of ice heave past booming, grinding, and thumping.

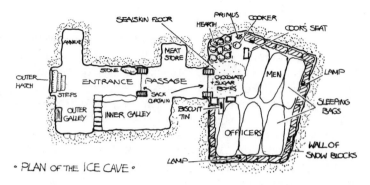

• PLAN OF THE ICE CAVE •

ICE CAVE

If plans went wrong and men were marooned somewhere in Antarctica their chance of surviving depended on being able to find animals for food and fuel. Animals lived along the coasts but almost all left at the end of summer to live out in the pack ice.

Six men were waiting on a rocky beach in February 1912. Their ship was meant to be picking them up. But it hadn't arrived. Soon the dark days and terrible cold of winter would be here. They only had thin tents and summer clothes. They had to find food, fuel and proper shelter, fast.

The seals and penguins were swimming away but the men managed to kill enough to last several months. There was no problem about storing the meat. It froze instantly. Oil from seal and penguin blubber gave fuel for the cooking, and light for little lamps which they made out of meat tins and pieces of unravelled rope.

The men decided to hollow a home inside a large snow-drift. Chipping and hacking at the ice they made a cave just big enough for six sleeping bags and a cooking stove. It wasn't possible to stand up straight, and everything – clothes, bags, walls, floor, their hair and skin – was soon black and filthy from the cooking. But the never-ending winds couldn't get inside the cave, and now and then it was so warm the ice started melting in black greasy drips from the ceiling.

The floor was made of pebbles covered with dried sea-weed, seal skins and pieces of tent. Sometimes a hungry man reached down and added a handful of seaweed to his meal. It tasted of mould and the thousands of penguins which had tramped over it. But all food tasted of penguin, seal blubber, smoke, soot, and grease.

Meat for each meal had to be chipped off a frozen seal or penguin with the hammer and chisel used for collecting geological specimens. Shreds of meat flew in all directions. But they couldn't afford to waste any. So they scrabbled on the filthy floor in the dark cave collecting the fragments. A lot of other disgusting things got into the pot as well. But they were too hungry to worry.

Special treats helped pass the dreary weeks. Every Sunday each man had twelve sugar lumps, and twenty-five raisins on the last day of the month. Most days they had a biscuit each. The biscuits were broken. 'I kept one as a pattern,' said the scientist in charge of food. 'Then I fitted together pieces on top of it, like a jigsaw, to get a complete biscuit for everyone. We spent hours thinking of new ways to eat our biscuit and make it last.'

Most of the time the men lay in their sleeping bags trying to keep warm and forget about their hunger. They hadn't much energy for moving around and their clothes were thin and torn. The lamps gave very little light. In the dim cave the men in their sleeping bags looked like huge furry caterpillars. When the lamps were out the darkness was intense. They didn't read much because the smoke made their eyes hurt, but every night someone read from one of their few books. Every Saturday night they sang all the songs they knew, over and over, and every Sunday night all the hymns.

After seven months in the ice cave they escaped. Filthy and thin, they pulled their sledge along the coast and back to their base camp. Spring had come, the sun was shining, and they had survived, just.

The six men – a naval officer, a scientist, a doctor, and three sailors – were part of Captain Scott's Expedition of 1910–12. While they were struggling to keep alive in their ice cave, Scott and his four companions had died on the inland ice. There were no animals to kill for food and fuel away from the coast.

ICE FLOES

An ice floe is any piece of floating sea ice whose edges can be seen. Sometimes they are flat, sometimes crumpled and hummocky. Most of the pack ice is made up of ice floes, anything from a metre to several kilometres across. Some are salty, some nearly pure water, depending on how old they are and how they formed.

ICE SHEET

Antarctica is smothered by a stupendous sheet of ice. On average the ice is two thousand three hundred metres thick. The deepest ice is four thousand seven hundred and fifty metres, going down far below sea level.

The ice buries almost all the continent. Only two per cent of the surface is revealed.

The ice weighs a tremendous twenty-seven thousand million million tonnes. It has pressed much of the land surface down below sea level. If the ice melted the land would, over thousands of years, rise up again above water.

Antarctica's ice sheet holds an enormous amount of water. It contains two per cent of all the water on Earth. The volume of all this ice is thirty million cubic kilometres. It represents ninety per cent of the world's ice.

Antarctica's vast ice sheet makes it the world's highest continent, three times higher than any other. Its average height is two thousand three hundred metres. The average height of North America is seven hundred and twenty metres, and Australia three hundred and forty metres.

The ice probably began to form about twenty-five million years ago, and had covered the continent by fifteen million years ago. But the present ice sheet is thought to be about seven hundred thousand years old. The ice that formed before has already flowed into the sea.

The ice sheet is formed by layers of snow falling year after year. The weight of new snow squeezes the lower layers, packing the snow crystals tighter until they turn into glacier ice.

The ice in the ice sheet flows very slowly outwards from the centre of the continent and down towards the coast. Here the slopes are steeper and the rate of flow speeds up. The ice flows at the rate of a few metres a year to one hundred to two hundred metres. The ice also moves fastest at the surface and most slowly by the bed rock. It has been worked out that a piece of snow falling at the place furthest from all coasts would take one hundred thousand years to travel the one thousand nine hundred kilometres to the edge of the ice sheet.

ICE SHELVES

Ice shelves were a mystery to explorers. Awe-inspiring white cliffs of ice rose from the dark inky water. Glittering white plains of ice stretched inland. Were they part of the continent? Or were they afloat? Could you live on them? What would they be like to travel over?

The Ross Ice Shelf which spills into the Ross Sea was called the 'Barrier' because it blocked the way to the South Pole. When men tried travelling over it they found treacherous crevasses. The surface was furrowed with ridges (sastrugi). Blizzards swept across it. In autumn the temperatures fell disastrously fast. In summer the sun reflected off the snow in dazzling light. The Barrier exhausted men. It was bleak, barren, silent.

Ice shelves are afloat, although anchored to land on three sides and 'welded' here and there to hidden islands. But ice shelves are slabs of land ice. They are part of the great ice sheet that covers Antarctica, spilling down off the central plateau and out over the surrounding sea. They have two important boundaries – the hinge where the ice begins to float, and the ice front, where they break up into icebergs. Ice shelves are constantly being added to by ice from the inland ice sheet and snowfalls. They are constantly losing ice by the calving of icebergs. If the adding and the losing stay equal, the ice shelves will be stable.

The ice shelves move slowly, endlessly. An American helicopter pilot searching for Admiral Richard Byrd's base on the Ross Ice Shelf saw a tent hanging from an ice cliff. The rest of the base had floated away on an iceberg. A dark line of rubbish could be seen two hundred and thirty centimetres below the surface. In eight years that much snow had accumulated.

Antarctica is fringed by ice shelves. The largest is the Ross Ice Shelf, a great triangle-shaped expanse of ice bigger than France. Five ice streams feed into it and seven major glaciers. The second largest, the Ronne Ice Shelf, is edged by the Weddell Sea. The thickness of ice shelves varies. The Ross Ice Shelf is nine hundred metres thick where it starts to float, and two hundred metres thick where it breaks up into icebergs.

Ice shelves are deserts. Nothing lives on them except the occasional human and visiting skua gull. But in 1977 TV cameras were pushed down a hole drilled through the Ross Ice Shelf. The camera filmed tiny animals swimming about the sea floor. The hole was four hundred and fifty kilometres from the open water.

ICE STREAM

Streams of ice flow through the ice sheet a bit like rivers. They flow fast, for ice. These streams can be fifty kilometres wide, and move one thousand kilometres a year. Sometimes the streams speed up and flow even faster. Is Antarctica's ice pouring away through them? What happens to Antarctica's ice is so important to the rest of the world that much research is being done to find out more about ice streams.

INTERNATIONAL GEOPHYSICAL YEAR, IGY

Antarctica was invaded in 1957–58 by over five thousand people, from sixty-seven countries. New bases were set up and old ones reopened on the continent and surrounding islands. Antarctica and outer space had been declared areas of special study for the International Geophysical Year. Twelve countries with political interests in Antarctica – Argentina, Australia, Belgium, Chile, France, Great Britain, Japan, New Zealand, Norway, South Africa, the USA, and the USSR – organized research programmes in the physical sciences. How thick was the ice sheet? Was it growing or shrinking? What lay under it? Was Antarctica two continents or one? How did the ice in Antarctica affect the world's weather?

Nations which disagreed in their politics or their claims on Antarctica managed to work together on scientific research. This co-operation helped create the Antarctic Treaty.

MACQUARIE ISLAND

ISLANDS

A number of small lonely islands poke out of the Southern Ocean. Some are joined to the Antarctic continent by permanent ice. Some, like the South Shetlands, are just off the coast. Some, like South Georgia, are near the Antarctic Convergence, windswept and fog-bound, with ice caps and glaciers. Some are further north with ice-free coasts, like Macquarie Island.

All the islands are important places for seals, and for penguins and other birds to breed. None had any humans living on them until sealers and whalers began arriving last century. Most islands now have imported plants and animals, introduced deliberately, or by accident. Some have permanent research and weather stations.

JAPAN

While Amundsen and Scott were trying to reach the South Pole the first Japanese Antarctic Expedition arrived in a small whaler, the *Kainan Maru* ('Opener up of the South'). Men landed and explored, and the leader Lieutenant Shirase led a 'Dash Patrol' over the Ross Ice Shelf which managed to reach a little beyond 80° South on 28 January 1912.

After the Second World War Japan agreed never to claim any part of Antarctica. The Japanese were one of the original signers of the Antarctic Treaty. They have scientific bases in Antarctica, and are heavily involved in fishing for krill.

KILLER WHALE

Killer whales like warm-blooded food best. All summer they cruise amongst the ice, snorting and blowing, their big black and white bodies gleaming. They poke their huge heads above the water and check for prey. Their sharp teeth crunch seals, penguins, fish. They like other whales – especially the tongues.

Early one morning in January 1911, men were unloading their ship. Two dogs were on an ice floe, tied up to the ship's rope. Six killers swam past. The tall black triangles of their fins rose above the water, then they dived. The photographer ran to the edge of the floe ready to take a picture. The next moment the floe shuddered, then rocked violently. Booming noises came from under the ice. The whales worked together, rising up under the floe and hitting it with their huge backs. Suddenly the floe lifted, then split. The whales reared up out of the water and looked about. 'One after another,' wrote

Captain Scott, who was watching, horrified, 'their huge hideous heads shot vertically into the air through the cracks which they had made. It was possible to see their small glistening eyes, and their terrible array of teeth.'

By amazing chance the dogs had not been thrown into the water. They stood on separate pieces of ice whimpering with fear and straining at their chains. The photographer raced slipping and falling back to the ship. The dogs were rescued. Even the tins of precious petrol stacked on the floe were saved.

Killer whales co-operate with each other, often hunting in packs. One explorer saw a line of killers with a leader out in front, which seemed to give a signal. The whales swam towards an ice floe. Just before they reached it they turned aside, creating a wave which washed the seals resting on the ice off into the water.

A killer whale is about the size and weight of a bus – ten metres long, and weighing eight tonnes. Killers are found in all oceans of the world, but some spend all their lives in the Antarctic. They live in family groups of four generations. Often the same group stays together for twenty years.

KRILL

Antarctic krill have to work very hard to stay alive. They hover in the water paddling furiously with their ten legs while they shovel microscopic plants into their stomachs. If they stop they fall, too heavy to float, down into deep water where they suffocate from lack of oxygen.

But while they are busy paddling and shovelling these small shrimp-like creatures are eaten by larger animals. Fish, squid, birds, penguins, seals, and whales. All feed on krill. Now humans have added themselves to the list. Ships scoop tons of krill out of the water at a time. Krill are high in protein although they have too much fluoride in their shells. Russians and Japanese take the greatest number and are busy developing new products from the animal and its shell. Four hundred thousand tonnes of krill were fished in 1989.

But the six centimetre-long krill is the most important creature in Antarctic waters. It is the centre of a food web which stretches through the oceans. Humans have over-exploited Antarctic whales, seals, and fish. Great care has to be taken not to do the same with krill.

During the cold dark months of winter, krill are hidden beneath the ice. They may scrape algae off the underneath of the ice and eat it, or they may live on the food they ate in summer. They are very sensitive to pollution. They need exactly the right amount of oxygen in the water. No one has yet managed to get captive krill to breed.

Antarctic krill gather in great swarms – nineteen million per square kilometre – feeding off the rich soup of tiny plants that grow in the warmth and light of summer. The ocean seethes and turns red with their leaping bodies. It is reckoned that there are six hundred thousand million million Antarctic krill, which means they might be the most numerous animal species on Earth. And scientists think that a krill – if it isn't eaten – can live to be seven years old.

LAKES

Large lakes lie three to four kilometres down beneath the Antarctic ice sheet. So far seventeen have been found by using radar sounding devices. They might have formed millions of years ago. It is even possible that something lives in the lakes. Scientists have found microbes surviving in the ice sheet which are tens of thousands of years old.

In the Dry Valleys in Victoria Land there are strange lakes saltier than the sea. The centre of Lake Vanda is a permanent block of ice. But far below the ice the temperature of the salty water is 25°C, like a tepid bath.

LATITUDE

Lines of longitude run between the North and South Poles like segments in an orange. Lines of latitude run around the Earth all the same distance apart. The two sets of invisible lines are like a net drawn over the surface of the Earth. They are divided into 'degrees' and help us fix our position anywhere on Earth's surface.

Latitude is measured from the Equator. One degree south (1° South) is just off the Equator. Ninety degrees south (90° South) is exactly the South Pole.

Latitude became a kind of score in the Antarctic. The oceans surrounding Antarctica are the world's stormiest and wildest. Sailors talked about surviving the 'roaring forties', the 'furious fifties', and the 'shrieking sixties'.

All of the Antarctic Continent lies below 60°S. In the northern half of the world there are cities, farms, and railways at 60°N. But here in the south, icebergs float in the sea.

Men competed to get the furthest south. Captain Ross' score of 78°S in 1841 was not beaten for fifty-nine years. Competing began on land as explorers edged towards the Pole. They liked to measure their progress in degrees of latitude. It made the journeys in the great frozen waste of Antarctica seem a little more bearable.

LEOPARD SEALS

Penguins line up on the ice to get back into the water. But none of them jump in. They shove, and push, and stare down. At last one penguin dives – or is pushed – and all the others follow, fast.

People watching the penguins thought they were playing a game. 'One by one they dived in at exactly the same spot . . . as if poured out of a bottle.' No one knew that down in the water a leopard seal might be lurking. If the first penguin into the water wasn't eaten the others knew it was safe to follow. This wasn't a game.

Leopard seals eat anything, from the little krill up to other seals, with penguins a favourite. They don't bother with tough penguin skin but jerk the bird out of its skin first. Long, sleek, fast animals, with a big spotted head and terrible razor-sharp teeth, they seem to hunt alone. There are probably two hundred and twenty thousand leopard seals in Antarctica and the islands.

MAGNETIC POLE

The magnetic Poles keep moving. Before you can get to them you have to work out where they are.

The North and South Magnetic Poles are the two points on the surface of the Earth where a compass needle stands vertically – straight up and down. But the Poles move surprisingly fast. At present they travel about ten to fifteen kilometres a year.

Captain James Clark Ross tried to reach the South Magnetic Pole in 1841. Ten years earlier he had stood at the North Magnetic Pole. But the South Magnetic Pole was high on the icy plateau of Antarctica. No human had ever travelled inland on the Antarctic continent and Ross had to give up.

The South Magnetic Pole was reached on 16 January 1909 by two geologists from Australia, Edgeworth David and Douglas Mawson, and a Scottish doctor, Alistair Mackay. None of them had travelled in Polar conditions before coming to the Antarctic.

Edgeworth David was fifty, a much-liked university professor. He felt the cold. He wears at least one singlet and one shirt, a Jaeger wool waistcoat, a wool sweater, a heavy blue felt coat lined with fleece, a heavy woollen pyjama coat, underpants, double sealed Burberry pants, a Burberry jacket, and on his head a fleece balaclava, a fleece-lined helmet, and a Burberry helmet, noted twenty-six-year-old Douglas Mawson in his private diary. The three men were sharing one large sleeping bag and Professor David and all his clothes took up more than half the space.

Sharing a sleeping bag had other problems. Mawson and Mackay were quicker than David and got into bed first. After a while David squeezed into the tent.

'He sits on our legs and faces,' noted Mawson. 'Finally . . . he struggles in all cold and bedaubed with snow . . . His pockets are full of food scraps, specimens, books, a tool set, etc.'

But the miseries of the shared sleeping bag were soon crowded out by other things. Dragging their two sledges weighing half a tonne through twisted, ridged, sticky sea ice was exhausting. They felt sick with the effort, and endlessly hungry, because they didn't have enough food. They crossed crevasse-filled glaciers.

'Crevasses found by falling in,' noted Mawson grimly. They reduced their equipment to one sledge and pulled it up a glacier to get on to the high plateau of Victoria Land. Here, frost-bitten, weak from lack of food, they pushed inland. The altitude made breathing difficult.

No one knew for certain the direction in which the South Magnetic Pole had moved. It wasn't where they had expected but they reached the correct area, according to calculations, on 16 January. It was just a point on the white icy plateau looking like all the others. They claimed the region for the British Empire, hoisted the flag, gave three cheers, and took a photograph.

The journey back was very hard and dangerous. Each man was suffering and the Professor was close to exhaustion.

'It took the lot of us to make a whole man,' Mawson wrote in his diary. Three days later he noted

'Prof's boots were frozen on . . . Mac now reports that his feet are more or less gangrenous. During most of the day the Prof has been walking on his ankles.'

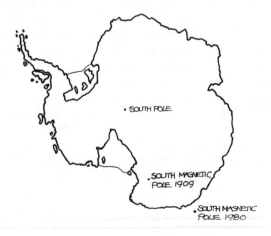

They hoped their ship would pick them up part way back. They were lucky. The ship found them, and took them home to base camp. They had walked two thousand three hundred and thirty kilometres in four months dragging a quarter to half a tonne of weight.

'It seems almost incredible,' wrote Amundsen, 'but these men succeeded in working their way on foot over sea-ice and land-ice, cracks and crevasses, hard snow and loose snow to the Magnetic Pole. What was better still, they all came back safe and sound.'

Some years later after doing more calculations David and Mawson worked out that they hadn't actually reached the true position of the South Magnetic Pole in 1909.

Today it is in the sea.

MAWSON

The sun was shining. The dogs were pulling the two sledges well. After the terrible country they had been through – the glaciers, the endless crevasses – this was smooth travelling. The three men relaxed. In a few days they would turn for home.

Xavier Mertz, Swiss ski champion, was ahead path-finding. Douglas Mawson saw him raise a ski stick, the signal to 'watch out' then go on. As Mawson came to the place he looked around but couldn't see anything. He jumped on his sledge and began working out their position on the map. The dogs pulled the sledge over the snow-covered lid of a crevasse. Mawson turned round and called out a warning to the young English army officer, 'Cherub' Ninnis, who was walking with his sledge just behind. The crevasse lid was no different from hundreds of others they had been over.

A few minutes later Mertz stopped and looked around, puzzled. Mawson turned. Where was Ninnis? Hurrying back he found a great gaping hole. Two sets of sledge tracks led up to the crevasse. Only one set carried on. He stared down into a black chasm. A chill draught hit his face. Far below on a ledge, forty-six metres down, he could see an injured dog whimpering. The crevasse plunged on below. There was no sign of Ninnis.

For three hours Mawson and Mertz hung over the edge of the crevasse, calling. Ninnis must have been killed instantly. The full horror of the catastrophe hit them. Ninnis had the strongest dogs. Their tent had been on his sledge, all the dogs' food and most of their food, the spade, and ice axe. They had ten days' food left, their sleeping bags, fuel, cooker, and a few clothes. They had been travelling for five hard weeks over appalling country. They were five hundred and ninety-three kilometres from base.

Mawson and Mertz fed the six remaining dogs some old boots, mitts and leather straps. They boiled food bags to make a thin soup for themselves. Then, on this sad day, 14 December 1912, they turned back.

A tiny cramped tent was made from a spare tent cover draped over Mertz' skis and a piece of broken sledge. They fried bits of tough dog meat on a metal lid. As each dog weakened it was killed and the two men and the remaining dogs shared it. Christmas Day was celebrated with dog stew and two bits of biscuit found in the bottom of Mawson's bag. The weather was bad, their clothes and sleeping bags were wet, they were famished and exhausted. But they were half-way home.

Then Mertz began to be ill. For a week they hardly travelled. Mawson tried pulling him on a sledge, and letting him rest. The skin was falling off their bodies, they were covered in blisters and scabs, their hair was dropping out, and Mertz got worse. Mawson knew that by staying with Mertz he was losing his chance of surviving. Their food was running out. They were only one hundred and eighty-five kilometres from their base camp: so little for fit men, so far in their exhausted starving state. But he could not leave Mertz. He nursed him in the tiny tent and the precious hours slipped by. Then early in the morning of 8 January 1913 Mertz died.

Mawson was alone. It would have been easy to lie in the sleeping bag and stop struggling. The weather outside was cruel. But Mawson decided he must try and get as far as he could. He was the leader of the expedition. He hacked the sledge in half with his penknife making it lighter to pull. He threw away everything he could spare. By 11 January he was ready to set out. His feet were in an appalling state. The skin had come off the soles but Mawson bound it back on with bandages, put on six pairs of socks, and hoped. His toes and fingers were frost-bitten. He felt as if his body was rotting.

Mawson reached another crevasse-ridden glacier. The weather was awful. He could hardly see. Blundering on through thick snow Mawson suddenly found himself dangling on the end of a rope inside a crevasse, with the sledge above creeping slowly towards the edge. So this was the end. The sledge would crash down on his head and he would crash down into the darkness below.

Then the sledge stopped moving. It was cold in the crevasse. He didn't have gloves on, and his fingers were damaged. But there was a small chance. He hauled himself, struggling, resting, struggling again up the rope and out on to the edge of the crevasse. It gave way under his weight, and he fell again.

Mawson hung, turning slowly. Below was blackness. The end of the fighting, of hunger, and pain. His body was chilling fast. His strength had almost gone. Somehow he got the will for one last tremendous effort. Slowly he hauled himself up the rope. He got his feet out of the hole on to the snow, and lay exhausted for an hour.

Later, having put the tent up and cooked a little food, Mawson lay in his sleeping bag thinking. Could it be worth going on, endlessly hungry, knowing that he would only fall down another crevasse? If he slept, and rested, and ate all his food now, he would at least have a few happy days before he died. Then he had an idea. He made a rope ladder and tied one end to the sledge, the other to his body. Now he would at least be able to scramble up out of a crevasse.

And so Mawson went on, falling through the lids of crevasses, climbing out, dragging his sledge, his feet in agony, his stomach cramped with hunger, hardly able to see because the weather conditions were so bad. His hair came out in handfuls, his clothes were wet and frozen. Then, after twenty-one days of travelling alone, he found by amazing chance a bag of food left by a search party. He had missed them by six hours.

The ice was so slippery Mawson kept falling over. He had thrown away his crampons to save weight. Now he made more out of pieces of wood and screws taken out of equipment on the sledge. With the crampons on his feet he reached an ice cave used as a depot only nine kilometres from the base hut. Here was food and shelter. The weather closed in. Mawson ate, and slept, and made more crampons. After a week a lull in the weather let him tackle the final journey.

Mawson arrived on 8 February. The ship which was meant to take his Australian Antarctic Expedition home had just left. Six men had stayed in the hope of finding him. 'What a grand relief!' wrote Mawson in his diary. 'To have reached civilization after what appeared utterly impossible. What a feeling of gratitude!'

Mawson was a very sick man. He was a thin, sad shadow after his frightful ordeal. For weeks he followed the men around, not talking, just to be with other humans. The news that he was found was radioed out. In return he heard that Scott and his four companions had died nearly a year before.

Mawson had to spend another grim winter in Antarctica. He returned to Australia only months before the outbreak of the First World War which was to kill and injure so many of the men who had explored in the Antarctic. He came back to the ice as leader of two more expeditions, 1929 – 1931.

Mawson reckoned that he was saved from the crevasse which took Ninnis' life because he was sitting on a sledge which distributed his weight. Ninnis was walking so his weight was concentrated on his feet. Years later it was worked out that Mawson and Mertz had suffered from Vitamin A poisoning because of eating dogs' livers.

METEORITES

The rocks which astronauts brought back from the Moon were examined in special sterile laboratories. Now rocks from Antarctica are treated the same way. Each is picked up by forceps, put in a dust-free sterile bag, sealed, and sent, frozen, to laboratories in the USA, Europe, or Japan.

The rocks are meteorites. Only two thousand meteorites had been collected in the world before 1969. Since then ten thousand have been found on Antarctic ice fields, in superb condition. 'It's a big Easter egg hunt for grown ups,' said a scientist. 'They're just lying on the surface.' Meteorites which have fallen over hundreds of thousands of years are gathered together in certain places by movements in the ice sheet.

Scientists study Antarctica's meteorites to find new clues about how our planet and the solar system began. The more we have, the better. Meteorites bring us invaluable news from space.

MIDWINTER DAY

On Midwinter Day in Antarctica, 21 June, the sun is furthest away and the darkness is greatest. It's a special holiday. Often it is celebrated as Christmas as well. The next day the sun begins its journey back, and winter is more than half-way through.

For the first explorers there were feasts, drinking, crackers, singing. Huts were decorated with flags. Men opened presents brought all the way from home. Special treats were unwrapped – tins of sweets, crystallized fruit, cigars, chocolates.

On Midwinter Day 1911 the men in the hut at Cape Evans with Scott ate seal soup, roast beef, Yorkshire pudding, tinned brussels sprouts and potatoes, followed by a flaming plum pudding, hot mince pies, raspberry jellies, pineapple custards, and champagne. A surprise Christmas tree was carried in with leaves of coloured paper and skua feathers. Toys for everyone hung from its bamboo branches. Then came a picture show of Antarctic photographs, followed by rum punch, games, singing and dancing. At 1.00 a.m. a man was found asleep in the snow in his underclothes. The temperature was 40°C below zero.

A wonderful aurora began. People stood outside in the clear hard night, away from the party. The ice creaked and groaned. The glaciers shone silver against the blue-black sky. Overhead the aurora unfolded, wave upon wave of gold, orange, and green light moving across the sky.

MINING

It's difficult to get at Antarctica's rocks to see if they have anything worth taking. Very few show. Most are jammed under thousands of metres of ice.

This hasn't stopped people hoping. All other continents have minerals; so why shouldn't Antarctica?

But if minerals, oil, and gas are discovered in Antarctica, there are big problems. Who do these resources belong to? And how can they be removed? Antarctica is hostile and remote, with exceptionally difficult ice conditions. Should they be removed? Antarctica is fragile and easily damaged. Oil spills and industrial pollution could be catastrophic.

The Antarctic Treaty avoided the difficult subject of natural resources, but governments have been discussing the problems of mining and drilling. Some argue that Antarctica must be protected. No mining or drilling should be allowed. There should be a permanent ban. Some argue that Antarctic conditions are so harsh and difficult that no mining is likely to take place, but regulations should be agreed on to control damage. And some argue that we cannot afford to ignore any resources wherever they are.

So far not a great deal has been found. There are seams of poor quality coal and low-grade iron. Traces of many minerals have been discovered. Natural gas has been detected. No oil has been reported although geologists feel sure it is there.

Mining and the exploitation of oil are thought by many people to be the most serious threats hanging over Antarctica. The international agreement to work peacefully in Antarctica would probably collapse if even one nation started taking minerals or oil from the continent. The Antarctic Treaty nations agreed in 1991 to ask their governments to ban commercial mining in Antarctica for fifty years.

MIRAGES

Antarctica's air is so cold, dry and free of dust there is no haze. Things far away can look closer than they are. And things appear which are not there at all. Antarctic mirages are very confusing. 'Icebergs hang upside down in the sky,' wrote Shackleton, 'land appears as cloud. Cloud-banks look like land.' The mirages happen because a layer of denser cold air refracts light beams.

MOUNTAINS

Antarctica has massive ranges of mountains. Some are completely hidden below the ice. Others rise up, immense walls of rock, cut by mighty glaciers. Amundsen discovered a range of mountains on his way to the South Pole in 1911. As a Norwegian he was

used to rock and ice. But he was amazed by the gigantic size of these mountains, 'glittering white, shining blue, raven black . . . pinnacle after pinnacle, peak after peak, crevassed, as wild as any land on our globe . . .'

Amundsen's range was part of the Transantarctic Mountains, one of the world's longest mountain chains. They cross the continent from the Ross Sea to the Weddell Sea. The mountains hold back the great ice sheet which covers the centre of Antarctica, like a dam holding back water. The ice breaks through the mountains in mighty glaciers which slowly spill down towards the ocean.

The Transantarctic Mountains divide Antarctica into two separate parts each with its own ice sheet. They also divide the continent geologically with the oldest rocks by far in the side facing Australia.

Antarctica's highest mountain is the Vinson Massif in the Ellsworth Mountains, five thousand one hundred and forty metres above sea level.

Mountaineers see Antarctica's mountains as the last real challenges left in the world to climb.

MOUNT BETTY

Back home in Norway Roald Amundsen had a housekeeper called Betty. She knitted warm vests for all the men on his expedition. She looked after him and he was very fond of her. He named a rocky peak after her in Antarctica. On the journey back from the South Pole, in January 1912, Amundsen's men piled stones up into a cairn at Mount Betty, and put a small package inside.

Seventeen years later, American geologists were exploring the mountains. They discovered the cairn made by Amundsen's men and excitedly opened the package. They found some paraffin, a box of matches and a tin. Inside the tin was a page torn from Amundsen's notebook. 'We have successfully reached the South Pole,' it read. 'Passed this place on the return . . . Everybody well.'

MOUNT EREBUS

The first men to climb Mount Erebus had home-made crampons strapped on to their soft reindeer-skin boots to give a grip on the ice. Slipping and scrambling, they dragged their sledge half-way up the mountain. On the third morning they left the sledge and as much of the heavy gear as possible and tramped on up carrying sleeping bags, food and cooking things in awkward bundles. That night they slept out in the open, at two thousand six hundred and fifty metres and −11°C. A blizzard began. For thirty hours they lay in their sleeping bags with the tent canvas folded over their heads while the wind roared and drift snow whirled thickly past.

On the sixth day, in the morning of 10 March 1908, they peered over the edge of the crater on the top of Mount Erebus. The air

stank of sulphur. The ground beneath them hissed and boomed. Far below inside the crater they could see openings out of which dense clouds of steam poured up into the sky.

They got home very fast by sliding down the icy slopes of the mountain on their backsides, using ice axes as brakes. There were two Australian geologists, two doctors, one naval officer and an English aristocrat. Their leader, Ernest Shackleton, was delighted. He wanted his expedition to be the first to reach the South Pole, and the Magnetic Pole. It had begun by being first up Mount Erebus.

Mount Erebus, three thousand seven hundred and ninety-four metres high, is Antarctica's most famous active volcano. A cloud of steam streams from its summit high into the air. Situated on Ross Island in McMurdo Sound it rises behind the bases of America, New Zealand, and Greenpeace, and the famous huts used by the men of Scott's and Shackleton's expeditions early in the century.

MUMMIFIED ANIMALS

Dead seals lie on the ground in one of Antarctica's strange dry valleys. They are far from the sea. No one knows how or why they got here. They are mummified, preserved in the cold dry Antarctic air. Some have been here for five thousand years.

Outside Scott's hut at Cape Evans a mummified husky dog lies, teeth bared, the leather collar still around its neck.

NANSEN

Fridtjof Nansen never went to Antarctica. But he influenced everybody who did. He was a great Polar explorer and scientist who in 1895 got closer than anyone before to reaching the North Pole.

Nansen worked out modern techniques for Polar exploration. He learnt from the people who lived in frozen northern countries and adapted their methods. Nansen believed in wearing properly designed clothing and eating nutritionally balanced meals. He believed in using skis, and dogs to pull sledges. He designed an efficient cooker to use on journeys, and a lightweight flexible sledge. He had a ship built for Polar work, the *Fram*, designed like a walnut to rise above the pressure of ice.

Many men who wanted to explore Antarctica travelled to Norway to ask Nansen's advice.

NORDENSKJÖLD

Otto Nordenskjöld's expedition didn't work out as he had planned. He and five men spent two years on an island off the Antarctic Peninsula waiting for their ship to pick them up. But their ship had been crushed in the ice. The twenty men on board escaped across the ice floes to another island where they built a hut of stones, ate penguins, and survived the winter. A third group of men waiting to be picked up built a hut of stones and pitched their tent inside. They also managed to survive the winter.

Men from all three groups met up after extraordinary and difficult journeys across the sea ice. And everyone (except one man who died) was saved by a rescue ship from Argentina in 1903. Much good scientific work was done despite the terrible difficulties. Nordenskjöld made a successful long sledge journey with dogs. The fossilized remains of a giant penguin were found. This Swedish expedition had men who understood how to survive freezing weather, but Antarctica's harshness defeated even their careful plans.

NUCLEAR POWER

The Americans brought a nuclear power plant to their base at McMurdo in 1962 to provide heat and power. They felt very enthusiastic. Nicknamed 'Nukey Poo' it was built in a hillside near the active volcano Mount Erebus. But it broke down. It leaked. In 1972 it was shut down.

Fuel is very expensive in Antarctica. But the nuclear power plant was even more expensive. As the Antarctic Treaty bans the disposal of nuclear waste in Antarctica, thirteen thousand tonnes of dismantled reactor and contaminated soil and rock had to be shipped back to the United States.

NUNATAK

Little islands of rock sometimes stick up above the white surface of Antarctica. These spires or ridges of rock are called nunataks from 'nuna' which means lonely and 'tak' which means jagged peak in Inuit (Eskimo). But underneath the snow are the sides of buried mountains. Nunataks are all that show.

OLD POLE

Deep under the snow near the South Pole is a hidden town, dark, eerie, and empty. The snow is slowly crushing the ceilings and buckling the floors. The temperature is −50°C in the silent passages and once-busy rooms of the first American base at the South Pole. Built in 1957 it slowly sank under its own weight and heat into the ice below, and slowly began sliding, with the great ice cap it is buried in, away from the Pole.

It is illegal to go down the long icy shaft into Old Pole now. It is too dangerous to enter the creaking rooms slowly crushing under the weight of ice. But people do. They go to salvage equipment and bring up bits of frozen food; and they go to see a piece of Antarctic history.

THE AMERICAN AMUNDSEN SCOTT BASE

OZONE HOLE

Ultraviolet light, dangerous to living things, radiates out from the sun. But our planet has a protective layer of gas, called ozone, which is able to absorb ultraviolet light. The ozone is spread very very thinly through the atmosphere from about fifteen to forty kilometres above Earth.

This vital invisible shield is being attacked and destroyed by chemicals in CFCs (chlorofluorocarbons) used in aerosols, refrigeration, air-conditioning, fast food cartons, upholstery padding, cavity wall insulation and solvents. The chemicals are very stable. Slowly but surely they work their way up through the atmosphere, breaking down in the stratosphere to release active chlorine. Each atom of chlorine can destroy hundreds of thousands of molecules of ozone.

The damage was first discovered in the 1980s by British scientists in Antarctica studying the ozone layer. So much destruction of ozone takes place over Antarctica that a 'hole' appears every spring, recovering in summer. In October 1987 most of the ozone between fourteen and twenty kilometres disappeared altogether. High flying American aircraft equipped with measuring devices flew into the stratosphere in 1987 and proved that chlorine released from CFCs was responsible. The ozone layer is also thinning over the Arctic. Satellites carrying a scanner make clear global maps of the ozone holes forming and recovering.

The scientific work carried out in Antarctica has been vital in discovering the effect of what were thought to be harmless CFCs.

PACK ICE

Pack ice surrounds Antarctica like a great white belt. Sometimes ships slip through quite easily following cracks of open water between ice floes. Sometimes the pack ice slams shut around a ship gripping it tightly. Occasionally the ice grinds and squeezes so hard it crushes a ship to death.

At the end of summer the pack ice covers just over a tenth of the Southern Ocean. In winter it grows and spreads and thickens, until it covers over half the ocean. Pack ice is a mixture of floating ice and open water, but the patterns of ice and water keep changing. Storms drive floes on top of each other. The ice can jerk on end under enormous pressure. The pack ice is always drifting with ocean currents and winds. It is always dangerous to humans.

Explorers sailing south were excited to see the beginning of the pack ice. This was Antarctica's wall. How long would they take to get through? There was no way of knowing. They tried to read the signs. A dark grey 'water sky' meant open water ahead. 'Ice blink' – white glare on clouds – meant ice ahead.

Scott's ship *Terra Nova* entered the pack on Friday 9 December 1910. Great bergs soon surrounded us, wrote *Dr Edward Wilson*.

'We were at once in still water . . . the soft seething noise of moving ice and an occasional bump and grating noise along the ship's side . . . We met our first two Adélie penguins on a floe . . . and flocks of Antarctic petrels . . . all asleep together on the top of some immense tabular berg . . . We saw the enormous blow of a great many huge blue whales . . .

Sat 10 Dec We entered some very heavy pack – very thick ice, and large pieces . . . seals turn up, lying asleep on floes.

Sun 11 Dec Today we are stuck fast in the pack . . . We all got our ski out and had some exercise on a very large ice floe . . . We are now within the Antarctic Circle. The sunlight at midnight in the pack is perfectly wonderful. One looks out upon endless fields of broken ice, all violet and purple

in the low shadows, and all gold and orange and rose-red
on the broken edges which catch the light, while the sky is
emerald green and salmon pink, reflected in the pools of
absolutely still water which here and there lie between the
ice floes. Now and again a penguin cries out in the stillness.'

In summer the pack ice is full of life. No one knew until
recently that many animals use the winter pack ice as well.

PEMMICAN

Pemmican is a mixture of dried beef, ground to a powder, and beef
fat. It was brought to Antarctica in tins and carried on sledging
expeditions in frozen lumps. The idea of pemmican came from
the North American Indians who pounded up dried buffalo or
caribou meat and mixed it to a paste with fat and berries.

'How greasy and thick it tastes at first!' said an explorer. 'And
yet how soon it seems to vanish.'

PENGUINS

Penguins are birds which have traded flying for swimming. Under
water they dart at speed using their tails as rudders and their
flippers like propellers. They take quick snatches of air, then
dive searching for krill or fish. Penguins find all their food in
the sea. They come on land to breed, change feathers (moult) and
rest.

On land they seem clumsy, waddling along on short legs. But
they can move fast by tobogganing on their stomachs, pushing
themselves with toes and flippers.

Penguins belong to the southern hemisphere. Six species breed
south of the Antarctic Convergence. There are Adélie penguins
by the million, the tall stately Emperor penguin, Chinstrap and
Gentoos, the big, handsome King penguin and huge numbers of
Macaroni with their bright yellow feathery eyebrows. They are all
well adapted to the cold, with thick, overlapping waterproof feathers and a layer of blubber.

Penguins are the most lively animals in Antarctica. Visitors find

them fascinating and funny. They appear so interested in everything, running up to investigate, seeming to greet humans with little bows. They look as if they are playing games of follow my leader and mountaineering on the ice.

But for penguins, life in the Antarctic is a struggle to find enough to eat, to avoid being eaten, and to raise their chicks.

PLANKTON

Microscopic plants grow over the underside of sea ice, staining it brown. In spring the ice begins to melt. The minute plants float off into the water where they grow so fast they form enormous thick soups, making the clear sea water murky.

These microscopic plants are eaten by vast numbers of tiny animals – the larvae of fish, sea slugs, snails, jellyfish, and krill. Together the plants and animals are called 'plankton'. The plants are 'phytoplankton' and the animals are 'zooplankton'. Antarctica's rich supplies of plankton attract enormous numbers of animals to feed.

PLANTS

Very few plants grow on the Antarctic continent. Ninety-eight per cent of the continent is permanently covered in ice and snow. But not much manages to survive even on the bits that are free. It's too cold, the winds are too dry, and there's not enough soil or water.

The only plants to survive are low-growing, small, or microscopic. Little patches of lichens grow on rocks. Some even survive on rock faces high on the Polar plateau. Lichens freeze in winter and recover very slowly in spring. Some mosses can survive under conditions nearly as severe as lichens. A few small liverworts grow on the west coast of the Antarctic Peninsula, with the continent's only two flowering plants, a grass and a pink.

Algae grows near the surface of some snow and ice staining it pink.

Plants grow very very slowly in these harsh conditions. They are easily damaged and take a long time to recover. A human footprint on moss shows years after it was made. Lichens increase only ten to sixteen millimetres in size every hundred years.

POLAR BEARS

There aren't any polar bears in Antarctica. The largest carnivore living permanently on the continent is a wingless midge which is only twelve millimetres long.

People expected to find fierce animals. The first men to spend a winter on the Antarctic continent took plenty of guns and boxes of cartridges to defend themselves. The boxes were found, years later, unopened.

THE POLE AT THE SOUTH POLE

The real South Pole doesn't move. The South Pole is a geographic spot on the Earth. It is a place where our planet spins on its axis and all the lines of longitude meet. It is the place where, however you turn, you always face north.

The South Pole is commemorated at the Amundsen-Scott Station by a large stripy pole with a silver ball on top, surrounded by the flags of the Treaty nations.

The real South Pole is near by. It is marked by a small, waist-high stripy pole with a knob on top sticking into the snow.

AMUNDSEN'S SOUTH POLE MARK . JAN 18, 1912

But the stripy pole moves. The ice below is slipping slowly towards the sea. Ten paces away from the South Pole marker is a metal post with a label. This is where the marker for the South Pole last year has already moved to. The ice at the pole moves about ten metres a year. The South Pole marker is hammered into a mighty slab of ice which is two thousand seven hundred and forty metres thick, and it is all slowly moving.

Very careful calculations have to be made to find out exactly where the South Pole is. There is nothing to show in the white expanse of ice. The first men to reach it, led by Amundsen, made a post by lashing together a pair of ski sticks and tied the Norwegian flag to the top. They planted it where they thought the South Pole was.

A month later Scott and his companions reached the area and left their flag. By the time the next men reached the Pole forty-four years later none of the flags and markers was there. Everything had been covered over with snow, and moved with the ice.

POLE OF INACCESSIBILITY

Powerful tractors with special wide treads dragged their heavy loads inland. High on the plateau the tractors sank in soft snow, their engines faltered in the thin air, and the men had difficulty breathing. The Russians were planning to build a base at the Pole of Inaccessibility, the place in the middle of Antarctica furthest from all coasts, for the International Geophysical Year. But they built 'Sovetskaya' six hundred and forty-eight kilometres short of their goal and five men were left to spend a grim, incredibly cold winter. Next summer, in 1959, they managed to reach the Pole of Inaccessibility and found that enough snow fell here each year to equal one centimetre of water – the same amount as falls on the Sahara desert. The ice was two thousand nine hundred metres thick over rocks only eight hundred metres above sea level.

PONIES

Several explorers brought small Siberian ponies to the Antarctic to drag loaded sledges across the snow.

The ponies needed much looking after. Their bulky food had to be brought to the Antarctic and carried on expeditions. They drank water which could only be obtained by heating snow, using valuable fuel. They sometimes sank to their bellies in snow. They suffered terribly in the cold, especially in blizzards. They were so heavy they were difficult to pull out of a crevasse, or the sea.

The Antarctic was not the right place for ponies. But the British explorers Shackleton and Scott believed in ponies, and depended on them in their plans to reach the South Pole.

PONIES WERE TAKEN BY THE GERMAN EXPLORER, FILCHNER, ON HIS 1911 EXPEDITION

RADIO

The first radio on the continent was used by Douglas Mawson in 1912. The first real user of radio was Richard Byrd. He took a professional announcer on his second expedition in 1933, who broadcast from a licensed station KFZ at the Little America base. Commercials, news, and amateur entertainments came direct to American homes from the Antarctic snow.

Once radio links were set up between Antarctic bases and the outside world the real isolation of Antarctica was broken for ever. Before radio, men who went south on expeditions were cut off from all contact with everyone else. Now they could hear the world's news, and know about their families. Expedition leaders could be in constant touch with their organizers and governments and listen to their advice.

RECIPES

How do you cook penguin breasts or seal brain? How about skua, pony or dog? At base camp there was usually a full-time cook and shelves of ingredients brought all the way from Europe. The cook baked bread, made sponge puddings, and turned seal into seven different dishes. But on a sledge trip everyone had to take turns at cooking. Most men had never cooked before. Hungry men eat anything to survive.

Here is a recipe for 'minced seal' from the notebook of Douglas Mawson, expedition to the South Magnetic Pole, November 1908.

'Very finely chop blubber in large quantity, fry in frying pan for long time, say half an hour at least, then add a lump of blood in amount up to a quarter of the meat to be used. Keep this stirring round as it thaws out. After the heat has cooked it to setting see that it is in fine state of division by pulverizing with spoon, then add meat (finer cut the better) in about equal amount with the original blubber. Add pepper and salt if needed. Stir frequently for about twenty minutes. If biscuit can be spared it will greatly improve the dish if added in powdered form enough to take up the oil.'

RIVERS

There is one river in Antarctica, called the Onyx. It flows inland. It starts in a glacier by the coast and ends thirty kilometres away in a frozen lake. It flows for a few weeks every summer. The rest of the year it is frozen.

PENGUINS' EGGS WERE A REGULAR AND POPULAR ITEM ON MANY EARLY ANTARCTIC MENUS - SUCH AS SCOTT'S 1901-4 EXPEDITION - BUT VERY FEW NATIVE CREATURES ARE EATEN TODAY.

ROCKS

Geologists came with the first expeditions to study Antarctica's rocks. They sometimes had difficulty finding enough rocks to work on. The biologists killed penguins to make stuffed birds for museums back home. Inside the penguins' stomachs they found little stones which they gave to the geologists to study.

Geologists have to work hard in Antarctica. But even one rock can be useful, and tell a great deal about when and how a piece of land formed. Geologists want to learn the history of our planet, and where Antarctica fits in; and whether the rocks of Antarctica contain valuable minerals.

ROSS

Captain James Clark Ross took two specially strengthened warships of the Royal Navy to the Antarctic. He planned to sail into the pack ice, which had stopped other explorers.

Ross chose a new area not on any maps and put his ships at the ice. *Erebus* and *Terror* forced their way through, jarring and crunching. On the fifth day, 9 January 1841, Ross was rewarded by an amazing sight. Ahead was open sea!

Ross sailed south but was stopped by land with magnificent ranges of snow-covered mountains. Great glaciers pushed out into the sea. He named a headland Cape Adare. Pack ice blocked the shore, so he landed on several small islands and took possession for Britain. He named his discovery Victoria Land after young Queen Victoria. On he sailed. Another astonishing sight appeared: a high, snow-covered volcano, with flame-lit smoke pouring from its crater. Ross began to wonder if he could sail all the way to the Pole. But white cliffs appeared stretching across their path. As they sailed closer the cliffs turned into a mighty wall of ice, sixty metres high, with a flat top, like a great slab sliced off at the sea. Ross realized that the huge flat-topped icebergs they had seen must have broken off this wall. Was it afloat? Did it rest on the seabed? Ross sailed along the edge of the ice-barrier looking for a break which would let him get further south. After three hundred and seventy kilometres he had to give up and turn back.

Ross had discovered the sea which is named after him. He had discovered the Great Barrier, now known as the Ross

'EREBUS' AND 'TERROR' WERE ALMOST WRECKED JUST AFTER CROSSING THE ANTARCTIC CIRCLE ON THEIR WAY HOME.

Ice Shelf. He had got further south than anyone else. He had discovered an active volcano which he named Mount Erebus, and mountains which turned out to be part of the Transantarctic Mountains. He had been lucky enough to find the one weak spot in Antarctica's defences. Ice loosens and moves out of the Ross Sea most summers.

Ross was an experienced Polar explorer. He went to the Arctic at the age of eighteen, and had been five times since. He was the first man to find and reach the North Magnetic Pole. Now he was under orders to find the South Magnetic Pole. He longed to put the British flag at both Magnetic Poles. After making careful measurements he discovered that the South Magnetic Pole was high up on his newly discovered Victoria Land. He could not find anywhere to get on shore. New ice was forming on the sea. He had to sail back north, to safety.

Next summer Ross tried to return to his sea. But this time the pack ice nearly stopped him. The little ships struggled with gales and fogs and took forty-seven days to get through. The third summer Ross decided to explore the Weddell Sea discovered by James Weddell twenty years before. But instead of Weddell's open sea he found pack ice so thick he had to give up.

James Clark Ross was called the handsomest man in the Royal Navy. When he returned home to England after four and a half years' exploring and scientific work, his fiancée's father made him sign an agreement that he would not go on any more Polar expeditions. Except for one little one, he never did.

ROSS SEALS

Ross seals live out in dense pack ice. So few were ever seen that they were thought to be very rare. Now we know there are perhaps a quarter of a million. They are the smallest Antarctic seal, only two hundred and thirty centimetres long, with thick blunt faces, small very sharp teeth, and large eyes.

SASTRUGI

Sastrugi are sharp ridges made by the wind in the snow surface. They may be small, like the ripples left by the sea in sand; they may be rough, like the furrows in a ploughed field; they may be iron-hard icy ridges higher than a man.

Crossing sastrugi can be exhausting. It's like climbing over a frozen sea. 'A day of sastrugi would leave us totally shattered,' said an expeditioner recently. 'It was all we could do to make camp, melt water, cook supper, and crawl into bed.'

SCIENCE AND SCIENTISTS

People have been measuring, testing, and probing the enormous continent of Antarctica ever since the very first visitors. Large numbers of scientists worked together here during the International Geophysical Year 1957–8. Scientists wanted to continue researching in Antarctica. An international committee was set up to co-ordinate scientific work. Today the Scientific Committee on Antarctic Research, SCAR, is the international scientific organization involved in the Antarctic.

Scientists study Antarctica's ice and water, air and rocks, animals and plants. Some scientists find out about Antarctica's resources for their governments. Others work for the reasons people have always worked, because they want to know more about the world. 'Why do we study seals?' asks an American doctor. 'Honestly. We study him just to find out how he works.'

Antarctica is a rare place. It is practically untouched by humans. There is much new information to be discovered. Antarctica is like a huge engine driving much of our planet's climate. It gives us a baseline for monitoring global change. Its ice holds vital information about our atmosphere and what is happening to it. The ozone hole was first discovered by scientists working in Antarctica.

Some scientists want Antarctica to remain a giant open-air laboratory, a place for scientific research which they argue is vital for the health and safety of all things that live on our Earth.

SCOTT

Robert Falcon Scott came to the Antarctic twice, the first time as leader of the National Antarctic Expedition in 1902, and the second as leader of his own expedition in 1911. He never left. He died on the journey back from the South Pole, only a day's travelling from a big depot of supplies.

But the supplies, like everything else on the inland ice, were frozen. Scott and his two companions Dr Edward Wilson and Birdie Bowers were travelling late in the exploring season. Winter was coming. The men were hungry, frostbitten, weak, and ill. They put up their little tent on 19 March 1912, and the next day a blizzard began. It blew the following day, and the day after. They couldn't travel in a blizzard. They had food for several days but no fuel to melt the snow for water.

They lay in their tent and one by one they died. The dates and the order are unknown. 'It is only sleep in the cold,' wrote Bowers to his mother.

Eight months later, in early summer, a search party saw the top of a tent sticking up out of the snow. They dug down and found the sleeping-bags with the bodies. They found the diaries and final letters written home. Then they put the snow back and left them where they died, with a cross made of skis.

The ice of the Barrier continued moving slowly towards the sea taking the bodies of Scott, Wilson and Bowers buried in it; and somewhere, also, the body of 'Titus' Oates who had died perhaps five days before the final camp, on his thirty-second birthday, and the body of Edgar Evans who had died a month before that.

No one knew if Scott had actually reached the South Pole until the diaries were read. Amongst the few possessions in the tent were a little camera and two rolls of film. Back at base one of the scientists tried developing the film. He was using chemicals that had been bought in England three years before, and equipment that had withstood two bitter Antarctic winters. The camera and film had been dragged on a sledge to the Pole and nearly back. It had been frozen under snow for eight months. The chances of seeing anything seemed very small.

But it worked. There, in the hut at Cape Evans, on the edge of the Ross Sea, the quiet sad survivors of Scott's expedition looked at the photographs their friends had taken at the South Pole. There was a picture of their rival Amundsen's little tent, with the Norwegian flag blowing. There were pictures of the five British explorers. Scott had written in his journal, 16 January 1912: 'The worst has happened. The Norwegians are first at the Pole . . . All dreams must go.' Cold, disappointed, weary faces stared out from the photographs. Their friends at Cape Evans could see the slight movement in Bowers' hand as he pulled the long thread which clicked the shutter.

In December 1912 the expedition ship *Terra Nova* arrived at Cape Evans and picked up all remaining men. On arrival in New Zealand no one on board was allowed to speak to anyone on land until the expedition news had been cabled through to England. A small launch kept buzzing around the *Terra Nova*, trying to get the men to talk. What's the news? Did you get there? Where's Captain Scott? Everyone on the ship stayed silent. As the launch turned to go a man called out: 'What kept you so long? Amundsen got to the Pole in a sardine tin!'

But the way people throughout the world reacted to Scott's death took everyone by surprise. Somehow the tragic near-miss seemed more important than Amundsen's success. Captain Scott became a hero. To everyone he was 'Scott of the Antarctic'.

Scott's base camp was set up at Cape Evans, Ross Island, in January 1911. Twenty-five men worked, ate, and slept in a wooden hut, with the sixteen officers and scientists divided from the sailors by a partition. Scott was a naval officer and he commanded the expedition as if he was on a ship. He had his own private room. There was a little dark-room for the photographer, and two tiny laboratories.

Scott planned to reach the Pole with sledges pulled by motors, ponies, dogs, and men. The motors failed. The Siberian ponies struggled in conditions they could not cope with.

The dogs did well, much better than Scott expected, but there were only enough to pull two sledges. He relied on men's strength. He brought a champion Norwegian skier to teach everyone how to ski but not everyone learned. Men hauling heavily loaded sledges over difficult surfaces in sub-zero temperatures need enough food. Food, and the fuel to cook it, is heavy to carry. Scott endlessly tried to work out how to carry more supplies. When blizzards kept men in their tents and they wasted vital days, when they lost their way, or someone was ill or injured, slowing the rate of travel, they went hungry.

Sixteen men, two motor sledges, ten ponies, twenty-three dogs, and twelve sledges left the hut in stages from 24 October, and were soon spread out in a long straggling line over the ice. By 9 December the Ross Ice Shelf had been crossed. The surviving ponies were shot as planned. The men began to climb up through the mountains three thousand metres to the Polar plateau. The dogs were sent back, in good condition; there was not enough food for them to continue. Twelve men in teams of four dragged the sledges up the

Beardmore Glacier, the route pioneered by Shackleton. It was desperate punishing work against the clock because each day spent on the journey meant a later return, in colder weather.

On 21 December, five hundred and seventy-four kilometres from the Pole, one team was sent back. On 4 January 1912, two hundred and seventy-eight kilometres from the Pole, Scott suddenly changed his plans. He added the strong Birdie Bowers to his team of four, and ordered Teddy Evans, Lashly and Crean to return one man short. Hauling as a party of five caused unforeseen problems. All food had been divided into four-man teams. Tents held four men. And Bowers had been ordered to leave behind his skis at an earlier depot. Now he had to work harder in the harness to keep up with his companions who were on skis. Bowers was very short. Plodding in deep snow was exhausting.

Scott hoped that Amundsen had not reached the Pole. The work was so hard, the margin of safety so narrow. He was risking everything on arriving first. When Amundsen's black marker flag was seen on 16 January surrounded by the paw marks of dogs, deep, bitter disappointment flooded the British. They found Amundsen's tent two days later, worked out by complex calculations where they thought the actual Pole was, then on 19 January turned north. Amundsen had begun his journey home a month before with fit dogs and many more food depots. Scott faced one thousand four hundred and eighty kilometres of man-hauling. The men were very tired, underfed and sad.

The big, strong sailor Taff Evans died, frost-bitten and delirious, at the bottom of the Beardmore Glacier on 17 February. Titus Oates walked out of the tent to die about 16 March, his feet frost-bitten and gangrenous. Polar explorers knew that illness or incapacity was a disaster. It was difficult to stop to help each other. By the time the three remaining men made their final camp, two hundred and thirty kilometres from the nearest possible help, Scott had a frost-bitten foot which had become gangrenous. It is almost certain that the men were suffering symptoms of scurvy, but the medical condition of the bodies which were found was never reported.

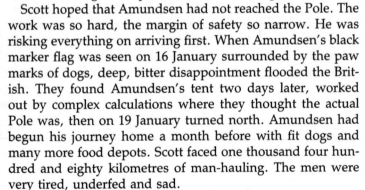

SCURVY

Sailors feared the dreadful disease scurvy. So did Polar explorers. Scurvy caused swollen, painful joints, softened bones, loose teeth, bleeding, and finally death. It was known that fresh food, fruit and vegetables, especially lemons, could get rid of scurvy. But explorers in the Antarctic brought their food with them, mostly tinned and dried. Many men did not like eating fresh seals and penguins. On exploring trips inland food was basic, with no chance of fresh food unless men ate the ponies or dogs which pulled their sledges.

Most doctors thought that scurvy was caused by something *in* food. Tins of food were checked to see if they were 'pure'. But scurvy was caused by something *lacking* in food – vitamin C. Only minute amounts of vitamins are needed by animals and humans to be healthy, but they are essential. Researchers began to find out about vitamins in this century.

Men suffering from the first symptoms of scurvy in the Antarctic felt colder, weaker, slower, and less able to concentrate. They walked painfully with swollen purple knee joints. Scurvy attacked towards the end of expeditions after months of eating dried and tinned food. Men with scurvy weren't able to cope with harsh travelling just when they needed all their strength to survive.

SEA ICE

Sea ice is all the ice in the sea. It is frozen sea water as well as the ice which comes from the land, mostly as icebergs. It is 'pack ice' which moves, and 'fast ice' which is solidly stuck to the seashore.

Every year the sea ice around Antarctica grows and shrinks. At the end of summer in March, four million kilometres of sea ice covers over eleven per cent of the Southern Ocean. In September at the end of winter twenty million square kilometres of sea ice covers fifty-seven per cent of the Southern Ocean. The ice cover has increased on average by about a hundred thousand square kilometres a day.

In March about eighteen million square kilometres of ice covers the Antarctic continent. In September, counting the sea ice, Antarctica almost doubles in size to thirty-four million square kilo-metres.

The growing and melting of the Antarctic sea ice is the largest seasonal process in the world's oceans. But it is also the very pulse of Antarctica. The sea ice affects everything that lives on or in the sea, from the smallest plankton to the largest whales. And it is crucial to humans.

The first explorers, sailors and scientists who came to the Ant-arctic were amazed by the power and size of the ice. But they did not understand it. They did not know when the sea would fill with ice and when it would go. The sea ice along the coasts is dangerous, treacherous stuff. Explorers watched it anxiously wondering when it was safe to walk on. As the days grow shorter and temperatures drop, the surface of the sea can suddenly be covered with ice. Needle-like crystals and flat crystals form under water. They float to the surface and freeze to each other in thin discs. Crystals shoot across, knitting the discs together until the surface of the water is covered in a jig-saw of little floes. The waves are squashed. White stillness stretches out from the land and ice seems to have conquered the sea. Then the wind comes and tears the covering away. The whole process begins again. And so it goes on until one day the sea is locked in ice.

In summer the explorers waited for the frozen sea to break up. If the ice did not go they would be marooned in the Antarctic for another year. Suddenly the ice starts moving. Cracks form. Lumps of ice heave in the ocean swell and long black tongues of water run between the floes as they split and crash and jostle out to sea on the tide. The sea seethes like a cauldron. Thick ice breaks apart as if it were glass. The sea is open again.

SEALERS

Seals were hunted for their fur, or for the oil in their thick layer of blubber.

Captain Cook reported that he saw seals and whales on his journey to the far south. As soon as they heard the news sealers from the United States and Britain set off to search.

Sealing was a bit like a gold rush. The first to arrive made the money. Men moved fast and kept their discoveries secret. Sealers wanted the valuable fur seal. They killed every animal they could. The next to arrive only got what was left. Colonies of seals were almost wiped out. The sealers had to keep moving on, searching for new supplies.

When no more fur seals could be found, men killed elephant seals for oil. Huge numbers of seals were slaughtered on the islands around Antarctica in the last century. The skins were sent north to China and Europe. The oil was carried back to light streets, houses and factories, and keep machinery working. When men ran out of seals they killed penguins.

Seals were easy to kill. Their enemies were in the water and they did not expect danger on land. Generation after generation of seals had been coming to the same rocky beaches to breed. Now suddenly humans appeared. The seals were not frightened or suspicious. In the water they moved fast. On land they were slow. The females were busy giving birth or looking after their pups.

The fur sealing 'gold rush' didn't last long. But seals continued to be hunted in Antarctica until this century. Elephant seals were hunted in South Georgia until 1964. A Convention for the Conservation of Seals, agreed in 1978, limited the number of seals that may be caught, and protected some species.

SEALS

Seals are mammals, warm-blooded, air-breathing animals like us. But three out of every five seals in the world live in the Antarctic on the ice and in water just above freezing.

Four species of seal are truly Antarctic – the crabeater, the leopard, the Ross and the Weddell.

The Antarctic suits seals. They have bristly hair and a layer of blubber under the skin to keep their body heat in. The sea around Antarctica has rich supplies of food. Seals look like huge fat floppy slugs as they lie on the ice. But in the water they are streamlined, agile and fast, excellent swimmers and hunters. Seals are successful animals. They have probably been around for twenty million years.

All baby seals are born in spring. The mothers come out of the water to give birth and feed their pups. The babies have been in a temperature of 37°C inside their mothers. Suddenly they are out in the cold air, maybe as low as −20°C. But they are born with furry coats and a layer of blubber and their mothers' rich milk helps them grow fast.

The early explorers killed seals for food.

'Poor seals,' wrote Edward Wilson in 1911, 'they have a very wretched time here when there's an expedition on the go.'

Seal meat kept many explorers alive, and fed their dogs.

Today scientists study seals to find out how they work. How do their bodies manage the cold? How do they find their way through the dark ocean under the ice? How do unborn babies manage the great changes of pressure as their mothers dive? Scientists have glued little computers to the fur of some seals. Every time they come up to breathe the computer sends information to a satellite where it is passed on to scientists in Europe and the United States.

SEISMOGRAPH

The shock waves from an earthquake happening anywhere in the world are picked up and recorded on seismographs in the American station at the South Pole. The seismographs can also detect an underground nuclear explosion happening anywhere in the world.

SEWING MACHINE

The winter snow drifted around Amundsen's little hut on the ice. The Norwegians tunnelled into the snow and dug out extra rooms. They made snow-cave workshops with work benches of ice, a laundry, a lavatory, and a little sewing room where Oscar Wisting worked every evening on his sewing machine. He made new tents, but the tent material was white. Amundsen wanted a dark colour to show against the snow, to rest the eyes and to absorb heat. So the tents were dyed blue with ink.

SHACKLETON

'We were camped on a piece of ice floe. An hour before midnight I felt uneasy. I don't know why. I left my tent and walked across the floe. Suddenly the ice cracked under my feet. It cracked right under the men's tent, and as the ice opened the canvas of the tent began stretching apart. I could hear muffled shouts as the men woke. The crack widened. I threw myself down at the edge. In the black water a whitish object was floating. It was a sleeping bag, with a man inside. I grabbed it, heaved, and got man and bag up on to the ice. Seconds later the edges of the ice crunched together with tremendous force. Then the crack opened again. Some of us were on one piece of rocking floe. The rest were on the other.

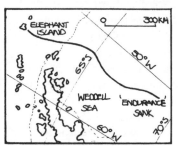

ROUTE TAKEN BY 'ENDURANCE' CREW TO ELEPHANT ISLAND

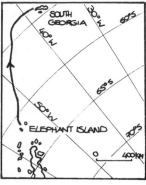

VOYAGE OF THE 'JAMES CAIRD'

115

There was no more sleep that night. We managed to scramble on to a flat piece of ice and huddled together, watching for more cracks. Killer whales hunted in the water between the ice floes. The night was very dark, with flurries of snow. Around 3 a.m. we lit the blubber stove and everyone had a hot drink. Then we began to feel a bit better.'

Twenty-eight men were standing on that floating lump of ice. Scientists, sailors, and Sir Ernest Shackleton, leader of a great expedition which planned to cross the Antarctic continent from one side to the other through the South Pole. But they had not even managed to set foot on land. A year and a quarter before their ship the *Endurance* had become trapped in sea ice. Helplessly they had drifted in a frozen world. Then, slowly, the ice started to destroy the ship. Twisting grinding ice snapped the strong wooden beams, burst the decks, forced through the cabins, shoved the engines aside. They carried as much food and equipment as they could save onto the ice, and watched as *Endurance*, squeezed and crushed, sank into the ocean. For the last six months they had been camping on the floes.

Now the drifting ice had brought them north to the edge of the great ice pack which surrounds Antarctica. Their floating home was breaking up in the ocean swell. Big gaps appeared between the ice floes. At last they could launch their three little boats and try to reach land.

Which land? There were no humans anywhere in Antarctica. Shackleton decided to aim for Elephant Island off the tip of the Antarctic Peninsula. No one had ever set foot on it. But the men were getting exhausted. Winter was coming. They must find shelter, and animals for food.

The men crouched miserably in the bottom of the boats. They were soaked, chilled to the bone, hungry, desperately thirsty, weary and sea-sick. Spray froze on the boats in lumps of ice which had to be chipped off with knives. Six days after leaving the ice floes they were alongside the rocky cliffs and massive glaciers of Elephant Island. Anxiously peering through driving snow for a safe place to land they saw a narrow beach below high cliffs. The boats were steered in through rocks and surf. Men lurched along the beach, laughing, letting handfuls of pebbles trickle between their fingers. Solid earth under their feet, after so long!

But Shackleton knew their problems were far from over. The beach wasn't safe. High tides could cover it. After a rest they must move.

Down the coast they found a long spit of bleak pebbly beach. Icy gales swept over it. Snow drifted against their few possessions. The fierce seas tossed sharp fragments of ice up towards the tents. But it was safe from the tide. Here Shackleton left his men to make a little hut under two of the boats and survive, if they could. He and the five fittest men were planning one of the bravest, most dangerous journeys ever made in a small boat. There were whaling stations on the lonely island of South Georgia, fifteen hundred kilometres away. If he could reach them, he had a chance of saving his men.

'When I walked through the blizzard to look at our boat she seemed to have shrunk,' said Shackleton. 'She was only an ordinary boat, twenty feet long. She had been dragged across ice floes, and survived a tough trip to the island. Now I asked our carpenter if he could do anything to strengthen her.'

Some frozen canvas was thawed out over the blubber stove then nailed across the top to make a cover. They would be able to crawl about underneath to cook and rest. Ice collected from a glacier was melted on the stove to fill water casks. On Monday 24 April 1916 the little *James Caird* set sail through great lumps of ice in a storm-swept sea.

From now on every hour was a battle. The men fought against the sea and against the winds; and they fought just to keep alive. They were passing through the world's wildest, stormiest ocean. They were chilled, sleepless, anxious. Their bodies hurt, their sodden clothes chafed their skin into raw sores. They finished the water and suffered agonies of thirst. Thirsty men cannot eat so they weakened from hunger. They faced gales, and one wave so gigantic, said Shackleton, that he had experienced nothing like it in twenty-six years of ocean voyaging. Somehow their boat lived through it, half full of water, sagging, shuddering under the blow, dazed by the attack. On the fourteenth day they caught a glimpse of black cliffs and felt incredibly happy. Then a terrible hurricane struck. It seemed as if nothing could save them from being wrecked. At the last moment, the wind shifted. On the sixteenth day, just as darkness came, they managed to beach their boat.

They were on the wrong side of the island. No one had ever walked inland from the coast of South Georgia, least of all tried to cross mountains and glaciers. But after food, water, and rest Shackleton and his men launched their little boat again, found a safe place for a camp, and prepared for the last amazing journey.

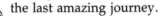

These men had been wearing the same filthy, worn-out, ragged clothes for months. Their fur sleeping bags were rubbed bald. Their tents were thin. Now Shackleton and the two strongest men, Worsley and Crean, faced a climb over unknown mountains. It was early winter. They tried to build a sledge but it was too heavy to pull. So they decided to travel with only the things they could carry. No tent, no sleeping bags, just a cooking stove, a lamp, a box of matches, an axe to cut footholds in the ice, one piece of rope, the log book of their journeys, and food for three days. Each man packed his food in a sock.

The three men set out before dawn on the fourth day after arriving. The full moon shone on the broken ice of the glaciers, the huge peaks of the mountains. They climbed and slipped, dodged and stumbled across glaciers, mountain passes, and inland ice fields for thirty-six hours. They did not dare sit down and sleep. That was the kind of sleep which passes quietly into death. They finally got onto the beach on the other side of the island by sliding down their rope through a nine-metre waterfall.

Ahead were houses with people, electric light, and news from the outside world. It was practically impossible to believe. Suddenly they realized how appalling they looked. They were filthy, ragged men with matted hair and long beards. Two small boys who saw them ran away fast in fear.

The Norwegians at the whaling station knew Shackleton well. He and his men had been mourned for dead. 'We not know three terrible-looking bearded men who walk into office off the mountainside,' said a whaler. 'Manager say "Who the hell are you?" and terrible bearded man in the centre of the three say very quietly, "My name is Shackleton." Me – I turn away and weep.'

They were safe. But it took Shackleton exhausting months and four attempts before he got a ship through the ice to Elephant Island to save the men he had left there. Everyone was still alive. The man in command, Frank Wild, had never given up hope. 'Whenever the sea was at all clear of ice he rolled up his sleeping bag and said: "Roll up your sleeping bags, boys; the boss may come today".' And so Shackleton did.

SHACKLETON'S PARTY SET SAIL FOR SOUTH GEORGIA IN 1916

SHIPS

Ships brought people to the Antarctic. They carried everything the people needed because nothing could be found in this hostile place. They provided home, and shelter, and comfort. They were the means of escape. Without a ship, men could not leave.

The ships that came to the Antarctic are almost as famous as the men who sailed in them. They were often very small. Sometimes they were most unsuitable for Polar seas. But usually they were tough wooden vessels designed for sealing or whaling in northern waters, and adapted for journeys south. Gradually men learnt how to strengthen ships to withstand ice. Wood was considered better able to stand the shocks of ice than metal. Engines were put in to provide extra power in the pack ice, although coal took up too much cargo space which meant ships could not travel as far as captains wanted. A few were built specially for their work of exploring.

Ships were appallingly battered and damaged in storms. They were driven against rocks and icebergs. Water froze over their decks, sails hung like iron sheets, ropes were solid lumps. There were extraordinary escapes, and remarkably few wrecks. A few ships were crushed in the pack ice and sank.

Ships could only get through to the Antarctic continent during the few months of summer. Ships delaying too long were trapped in the ice for the winter. In the 1950s powerful strengthened ice-breakers came to the Antarctic able to plough through the pack ice, turning huge ice floes aside, cracking and crushing the ice, forcing a passage for other ships to follow.

Today ships in the Antarctic have radar which can pick out the shape of an iceberg in fog, the hidden danger of ice under water. Before radar, ships moved through the hazards of Antarctic seas relying only on the eyes and experience of the crew.

SKUA

Skuas are big, bold, noisy birds. Life is hard in the Antarctic and skuas live off the weak. They often nest near penguin rookeries eating eggs and chicks. But they also eat fish, krill, and squid from the sea. They are good at forcing other birds to give up their carefully collected food. Sometimes they eat the birds as well. They also eat each other's eggs, and chicks. Skuas gather round the dead and dying, fighting over the pickings.

Skuas leave Antarctica for five months in winter. They are the first summer visitors to return, flying in from as far away as Britain, Japan, or Newfoundland. They nest all around the coast of the continent. But these powerful brown seabirds have been seen hundreds of kilometres inland towards the South Pole, which makes them the most southerly bird in the world.

Humans in Antarctica know the scavenging skua well. Skuas take anything they can get – belts, camera lenses, knife sheaths.

'It matters not what is left lying on the ice,' said one scientist, 'they will soon have tried to eat it or move it.'

Skuas have no fear of humans. Anyone coming near their nests is attacked. They circle slowly flying low, then come in fast straight for the head, whacking it with feet and wings.

But hungry people who eat skua eggs say they taste delicious. And skuas themselves are said to taste like duckling.

SLEDGE

The sledge used today was designed over a hundred years ago by Nansen for the Arctic. It is made of wood, light weight and strong, with two long runners shaped like skis. All parts are lashed together or joined with special wood-working joints, and no screws are used. A sledge three and a half metres long weighing twenty kilograms can carry half a tonne of weight. Modern runners are coated with fibreglass or plastic to reduce friction.

But a sledge does not move by itself. Something has to pull it. Today ski-doos are used. The engines of these 'tin dogs' only need feeding when they are in use. Some people still prefer real dogs which need feeding and looking after whether they are working or not. Great Antarctic journeys have been made with dog teams pulling sledges.

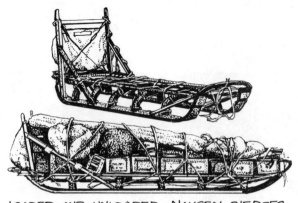

LOADED AND UNLOADED NANSEN SLEDGES

Some explorers used ponies to pull sledges. Dogs are meat-eaters thriving on seals. But ponies' food did not grow in Antarctica. Ponies had to eat bulky hay and oats, brought south in ships.

For many years British explorers relied on their own bodies as the power supply. They 'man-hauled' their sledges, harnessing themselves up and dragging the weight, taking the strain on their stomachs. Man-hauling was a slow, physically exhausting way of travelling.

SLEDGE PACKING

At the front of the sledge is a box, permanently tied on, with all the delicate scientific instruments, cameras, matches, and the lamp for the cooker inside. The cooker is tied on top. Behind is a large green canvas container fixed to the sledge. Inside are bags of food, each with enough food for a week. Behind this are two big tins each filled with two weeks' supply of sledging biscuits – eight biscuits a day each. Above is another green container holding the repair kit, and small bags with the four and a half kilograms of extra clothing each man is allowed to carry. At the back are tins of oil for cooking. On top of everything, making the load as even and smooth as possible, are the tent and tent poles, the shovel and ice axes, and the green canvas bag holding the food for the current week.

Raymond Priestley packing for a four-man geological expedition, 1911.

SLEEPING BAGS

Camping out in the Antarctic today means sleeping in a double layer sleeping bag, down on the outside, synthetic fur on the inside, on an inflated airbed, on a damp-proof ground sheet, inside a well-designed tent.

The first explorers used reindeer-skin sleeping bags. At night men closed the openings of their bags trying to keep warm. But the air inside the bags quickly became too stale to breathe. Reindeer hairs stuck in their nose and mouth. The ice in their clothes melted inside the bags, and warm, sodden reindeer-fur bags smelt nasty. Out in the open air the bags froze stiff as boards. Various ways of sleeping were tried: three men in the same large sleeping bag (a failure); sleeping with the hair on the inside; sleeping with the hair on the outside. Men had strong opinions about which was best.

TOM CREAN AND EDGAR EVANS OF SCOTT'S PARTY SEWING FUR SLEEPING BAGS, 1911.

SNOW

Snow in Antarctica isn't like other snow. It falls, in the very low temperatures, as fine dry powder or crystals so tiny you can only see them glinting against the sun. The air is so dry and cold that big, soft flakes cannot form. You can't make snowballs out of this snow. It's like sand, or flour, or dust, depending on the temperature. The colder the air the smaller each individual dot of snow. You can't leave a footprint once this snow has lain cold on the surface. It becomes hard and gritty like a stone. The best way of getting some of this snow it to saw it up into blocks. And the colour is the whitest white.

Snow which has already fallen is picked up and blown around the surface of the continent by endless winds. This wind-blown drift snow behaves rather like sand. It forms ridges and dunes, and cuts into surfaces eroding them.

So much drift snow is blown by a blizzard it's like being inside a heavy white sea. The snow gets into every crack of clothing, it works its way into the tiniest opening in a tent or a building, it even gets inside a watch.

SOUTHERN OCEAN

Antarctica is completely surrounded by a wide, deep, and exceptionally stormy ocean. This Southern Ocean forms one-tenth of all the world's oceans. But it is different from all others. The Southern Ocean has massive waves, enormous winds, and important currents. It is very cold, although in winter the sea is much warmer than the air above. The water is rich in oxygen, and extremely rich in all the chemicals needed by plants for healthy life. It supports an extraordinarily large number of living things. And it produces ice, which affects the water, influences all other oceans, and has a major effect on the world's climate.

The Antarctic continent lies in the centre of the Southern Ocean. For three-quarters of the year the sea surrounding Antarctica is frozen. For a couple of summer months, from December to early March, the edge of the ice retreats and breaks up. In winter more than half of the ocean is covered in ice. Even at the end of summer one-ninth is covered in ice.

The dangerous sea journey through the wild Southern Ocean helped keep Antarctica hidden from human visitors.

SOUTH POLE

At the South Pole the sun sets once in the year and rises once. The twilight and darkness last for six months from March to September. But even in summer when the sun never sets the temperature does not rise to freezing point. The highest temperature recorded so far is −21°C. The lowest is −83°C. The average for the year is −49°C.

The South Pole is high on the rounded plateau of central Antarctica, two thousand seven hundred and ninety-nine metres above sea level. The air is thin and dry, and it's easy to suffer from altitude sickness. The surface of the snow is rock hard. Ninety metres under the South Pole the snow turns into ice. The ice goes down for another two thousand six hundred and fifty metres before it grinds on the rock which is Antarctica.

SPORT

One dark afternoon in the winter of 1911 two men decided they needed exercise. They padded some woollen mitts with seaweed to make boxing gloves. They put two or three candles in a deserted hut to give some light. They stripped to their vests and began to box. But such thick clouds of steam rose from their bodies into the frozen air they couldn't see each other. After three minutes they had to stop and wait for the air to clear.

Football on the frozen ice was a popular sport in winter with early explorers. But it was difficult to see the ball in the gloom, and the ice was hard and rough to fall on.

Today there is even a golf course – on the ice – at the American base at McMurdo Sound.

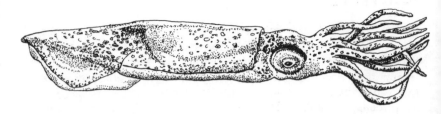

SQUID

We don't know much about the big-eyed, big-brained, jet-propelled squid. We know even less about the squid which live in Antarctic waters. We do know they feed on krill, fish, and each other. We know they are eaten by sea birds, seals, and whales – one estimate reckons thirty-four million tonnes of them each year, which means there must be a lot of squid in the southern oceans.

Squid grab their prey with tentacles and bite with their sharp beaks. Eighteen thousand squid beaks were once found inside the stomach of one sperm whale.

STINKERS

Come too close to a giant petrel's nest and it will aim a stream of foul-smelling sticky oil at you. Even a day-old chick crouched in the nest of feathers, bones, and stones can spit the oil.

Giant petrels are nicknamed 'stinkers' or 'stink-pots'. They feed on whatever they can scavenge in the tough Antarctic world – dead seals, other birds, and anything in the sea.

SUMMER

Where the sea meets the land, and the ice joins with the sea, most life happens in Antarctica. During summer with warmth and long hours of light the edge of Antarctica is busy with living things. Whales feed amongst the pack ice. Seals come on shore to have their pups. Birds nest wherever they can find a space. Millions of penguins lay their eggs. The sea seethes with krill and a rich soup of microscopic plants. Everywhere there are gaping mouths to fill, hard-working parents, the hunted, the hunting.

The length of summer depends on where you are, but the warmest months are November till February. Even then blizzards and harsh raking winds still blow. The temperature still mostly stays below freezing. But in some places, particularly on the Peninsula, it can rise above freezing, and that feels like shirtsleeves weather. Snow melts where there are rocks or gravelly beaches and the slush doesn't freeze till night. And as the days pass the sun sets and immediately rises until it rolls around the sky all twenty-four hours. Parts of Antarctica receive more sunlight than the Equator. Although the ice and snow reflect eighty per cent of the sun's heat, the light glares, hurting eyes and burning skin.

In summer the midnight sun is warm and bright. 'Every evening,' said a journalist, 'the sun looked as bright and fresh as if it had just risen.'

SWIMMING

The water is so cold in Antarctica it hurts. 'When you first get in it feels like someone's pushing on your head with a shovel,' said a biologist. Scientists swim in this freezing water to study animals in their natural habitat – krill, the creatures living on the sea floor, the seals and penguins. They wear dry suits with three layers of underwear. It takes an hour to get ready. But you need the hour to get your mind ready as well as your body.

Under the sea ice divers enter a beautiful blue-green world. The ice lid above glows softly bright. Little fronds of ice grow down from the bumpy underside of the ice. Seals swim by, their bodies smooth and fast. Penguins rocket past.

Some people swim in Antarctica to join exclusive swimming clubs. They wear nothing except their socks. Socks keep feet from sticking to the ice.

TENT

The special tent shaped like a pyramid used in the Antarctic was designed by an American, Dr Frederick Cook. Cook got the idea from the skin tents of Eskimos and the tepee of the American Indians. He tried his idea out while he was stuck all winter in Antarctic ice on board the *Belgica* in 1898.

Cook's tent could be put up easily, didn't weigh much, and could survive a gale. It had a skirt of extra material round the base on which snow could be piled to help hold it down. The pyramid tent has a door like a funnel which is tied up with a drawstring. The modern version has a built-in floor of weatherproof material, with trapdoors which can be lifted up to get clean snow for cooking, or to use as a lavatory when caught in a blizzard. An inner tent, providing a layer of insulating air, keeps the tent almost uncomfortably warm when the Primus stove is lit and roaring.

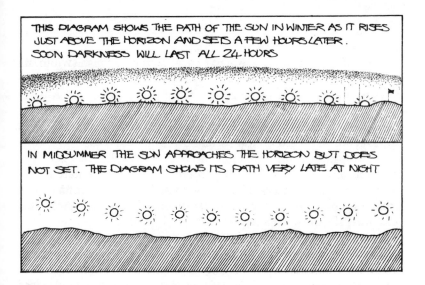

THIS DIAGRAM SHOWS THE PATH OF THE SUN IN WINTER AS IT RISES JUST ABOVE THE HORIZON AND SETS A FEW HOURS LATER. SOON DARKNESS WILL LAST ALL 24 HOURS

IN MIDSUMMER THE SUN APPROACHES THE HORIZON BUT DOES NOT SET. THE DIAGRAM SHOWS ITS PATH VERY LATE AT NIGHT

TIME

In Antarctica time zones crowd together. At the South Pole they all meet. You can if you want walk around the world in about five steps at the South Pole. You can also walk from today to tomorrow and back.

Each station in Antarctica decides which time zone to work in. But it does not really matter when people decide to sleep and work. In the middle of summer sunlight blazes in the windows at midnight and curtains are closed to keep the brightness away. Outside the sun rolls around the sky at about the same height day and night. In the middle of winter the sun does not rise and day happens in the dark.

TOURISTS

Antarctica is remote and harsh. Yet it has a wild beauty. The landscape is awe-inspiring, majestic. The air is pure, the silence profound. Many of those who have been there want to return. 'Would you go again?' the young Douglas Mawson was asked, over and over, after he returned from the hard journeys of Shackleton's Expedition in 1907–1909. 'No! No!' said Mawson. In two years he was back in Antarctica.

Most of us will never see Antarctica. Several thousand tourists travel there every summer on expensive cruises. Ships stop at research bases, historical sites and penguin rookeries. But Antarctica is a fragile environment, easily damaged by too many visitors. And Antarctica is dangerous. An aircraft carrying tourists on a sightseeing flight from New Zealand crashed into Mount Erebus in 1979 killing two hundred and fifty-seven people. If an accident happens to tourists in Antarctica there is no government organization to provide services. Help must come from the scientific bases where each summer a tight programme of research jostles for everyone's time and money.

But tourists cannot be prevented from coming to Antarctica. As well as the commercial tours there are increasing numbers of private visitors on small private expeditions to explore, study, paint, climb mountains, ski, and experience this great wilderness area. Perhaps each visitor will help spread knowledge of Antarctica and its special needs.

TRANS-ANTARCTIC EXPEDITIONS

After the South Pole was reached in 1911 the last great challenge in Antarctica seemed to be an overland journey across the continent from one side to the other through the Pole.

Shackleton's attempt in 1914–17 was a disaster. The next attempt used all the technology available. The Commonwealth Trans-Antarctic Expedition of Fuchs and Hillary, 1955–58, achieved the first successful crossing in ninety-nine days.

The second land crossing, 1980–81, was made in sixty-seven days by three men driving small sledge-pulling ski-doos. Sir Ranulph Fiennes, Charles Burton, and Oliver Shepard crossed Antarctica as part of their English Transglobe Expedition around the world via both Poles, 1979–82.

The third crossing of Antarctica used dogs hauling sledges, the same method of travel as Amundsen on his successful journey to the Pole seventy-seven years earlier. Six men, one each from the USA, Russia, France, UK, China, and Japan travelled the longest route from the tip of the Antarctic Peninsula to the Russian base Mirnyi via the Pole. This Trans-Antarctic Expedition, leader Will Steger (USA), achieved the six thousand-kilometre journey in seven months, in 1989–90. All forty dogs survived. 'Antarctica is a monster,' said an expeditioner at the end. 'It is not a playground. We are glad to be finished.'

TREES

'Not a tree was to be seen, nor a shrub even big enough to make a toothpick,' said Captain Cook when he discovered what he called the savage and horrible island of South Georgia.

No trees grow in Antarctica, or any of the islands in the Southern Ocean.

If South Georgia was moved to the same latitude in the northern hemisphere it would be in the north of England. But it has a climate like Greenland. The great expanse of the Southern Ocean makes conditions in the south much colder than in the north.

Trees did once grow in Antarctica. Fossil tree trunks and fossil leaves have been found, reminders of warmer climates in the past.

TRUE STORIES

Books about journeys to the Antarctic were very popular. People liked reading about adventures and heroic escapes. Leaders of the expeditions, and scientists, described their achievements. Their names, and all that they did, became well known. Books were also important publicity. Public money paid for many expeditions.

But the books told the good side. There was a kind of agreement between men who had suffered so much together – who lived cooped up in crowded winter quarters, who camped out in appalling conditions, who travelled long gruelling journeys – not to tell the inside stories. The stress on men in the Antarctic was enormous, especially in the early days. A few went mad. Some suffered from depression. Friends could turn into enemies. People's personal habits became unbearable. In conditions of physical suffering and constant danger men could be truly terrified, become aggressive, work hard and unselfishly for the good of everyone, or avoid work. Men doubted each other's judgements. They thought decisions made by their leaders wrong, or stupid. In many ways it was like wartime. As in war, men who had experienced much together clung together and great feelings of comradeship grew. Bad times weren't talked about.

Even letters home usually said only the good things. Men did not want their families worried or upset.

Many men kept a diary, but most were not truly private. If an explorer died he hoped his diary would be found with his record of achievements. Some diaries were written to be turned into books.

Occasionally men wrote what they truly felt in their diaries. A few put their private thoughts into code. Diaries and letters home were never meant to be published. But if they can be read today they give us some feeling of what it really must have been like. The books tell wonderful stories. Diaries and letters tell human stories. They are all part of a complicated truth.

VOSTOK

Vostok is the highest and coldest of all Antarctic bases. The lowest temperature ever recorded in the world happened here on 21 July 1983, −89.6°C. Established by the Russians in 1957 Vostok is three thousand four hundred and eighty-eight metres above sea level. But the ice Vostok sits on is three thousand seven hundred metres thick, which means the rock of the continent so far underneath it is actually below sea level.

The USSR has bases all around Antarctica, in almost everyone else's claimed territory. It is the largest national presence on the continent.

WATER

There is almost no running water on the Antarctic continent. Sometimes in summer snow thaws at the edge of the glaciers, or over black rocks, or sand. Otherwise all of Antarctica's vast supply of fresh water – nine-tenths of all the fresh water in the world – is held as ice or snow.

Dying of thirst is easy in this frozen continent. Ice and snow can't be drunk. Heat is necessary to melt it into water. A lot of snow (and heat) is needed to make a little water. Four cupfuls of snow make about one of water, depending on the type of snow.

Explorers living at a base camp had to make sure they kept a supply of clean snow to use as water. It was best to quarry the snow from underground. Today water is carefully rationed at bases. Fuel is so expensive that no more water is made than absolutely necessary. So in the cleanest land on Earth there isn't much washing. At the American base at McMurdo two two-minute showers are allowed per person per week.

WEATHER

Antarctica is the coldest, driest, windiest continent, surrounded by the stormiest sea. Its high central plateau is a freezing desert with an annual mean temperature of below −55°C. Less than five centimetres of water fall a year, as snow.

Around the coast temperatures are warmer, anything from −10° to −20°C. Six times more snow falls here than on the plateau. Powerful winds blow.

Antarctica has a great deal of cloud, fog, and severe blizzards, especially near the coast. But when the sky is clear, and the sun shines, the light is brilliant. The air is so clean and dry that distant things appear close and it is difficult to tell how far away anything is.

WEDDELL

James Weddell sailed in a sea which nobody since has been able to sail in so easily.

After searching for fur seals in the Antarctic islands Weddell decided to take his two small ships south. The *Jane* and *Beaufoy* battled through the usual gales, fogs, and floating ice. Suddenly

the weather improved. The ice disappeared. On 20 February 1823 Weddell was further south than anyone had ever been, and still the sea was clear, except for a couple of icebergs. The weather was mild. He could see no land.

Weddell had discovered a new sea which was later given his name. Only freak weather conditions allowed him to make the journey. The Weddell Sea is usually full of dangerous, difficult ice.

Weddell was very interested in science. He found a new species of seal which was also named after him.

WEDDELL SEAL

Weddells live further south than any other seal. During winter they live under the coastal ice of Antarctica. The cold above the surface is terrible. The sea is warmer. They dive as much as six hundred metres down into the dark, silent waters looking for fish and squid. But they have to keep their breathing holes in the ice open. Seals come up to breathe about every ten minutes although they can last for an hour. Weddells use their specially shaped front teeth and hinged jaws to chew upwards through the ice, sawing away at the edges of their holes. All the chewing and sawing wears their teeth down so Weddells only live for about twenty years. They can never be kept captive. They always try to carve the concrete sides of their pools, and die of dental infections.

In spring Weddells haul themselves out through tide cracks onto the inshore ice around Antarctica and lie snoozing in groups. Here the fat furry grey babies are born, one and a half metres long and weighing twenty-five to thirty kilograms. 'They sound like sheep and lambs bleating and baaing,' said an explorer. In five or six weeks they are swimming with their mothers.

Under water, Weddell seals make many sounds: whistles, gurgles, grunts, trills, hoots, and a 'musical moan'. 'If one lies down with one's ear on the ice one can generally hear them,' wrote a scientist at Cape Evans, in winter 1903.

Weddells are the best-known seals in the Antarctic. There are probably eight hundred thousand living on and under the coastal ice.

WHALES

Whales live in all oceans of the world. They come above the surface only to breathe, or look around, and occasionally to leap. They are mammals, like seals, and us, and their bodies are about the same temperature as humans'. But unlike seals, they give birth in the sea, and their babies suck milk under water.

The kind of food whales eat in Antarctic waters depends on the design of their mouths. One type of whale has teeth. The killer is the most famous toothed whale, hunting in packs along the ice eating anything it can catch. The largest toothed whale in the Antarctic is the massive-headed sperm whale. Only the mature males come south to feed. They can dive three kilometres down into the dark ocean depths, for up to an hour at a time, searching for large squid.

Whales without teeth have sieves in their mouths, horny filters hanging in rows called 'baleen'. Baleen whales use the Antarctic as a massive meal table. They come for the summer to feed and store up food. Then they swim back north to warmer water to mate, or give birth. Baleen whales feed on the smallest animals in the sea, plankton and krill. They gulp huge mouthfuls and force the water out through the sieves, trapping the minute creatures, or skim the food soup off the surface. Six species of baleen whale visit Antarctica in summer: the blue, minke, sei, southern right, humpback, and fin.

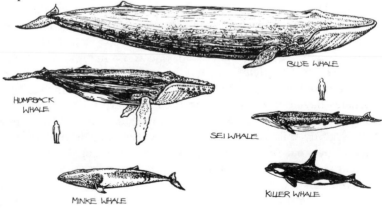

BLUE WHALE

HUMPBACK WHALE

SEI WHALE

MINKE WHALE

KILLER WHALE

◦ COMPARATIVE SIZES OF SOME ANTARCTIC WHALE SPECIES ◦

Whales eat a huge amount. It is reckoned that they take forty-three million tonnes of krill and six million tonnes of squid from Antarctic waters every year.

Whales were once land animals. Their leg bones have disappeared, their arms have turned into flippers. The remains of hairs sprout on some whales' faces. Their tails are horizontal, not vertical, as in fish. Like aeroplanes, they cannot go backwards; and like aeroplanes, their bodies are streamlined and smooth. Whales have a thick layer of blubber to protect them from the cold. But if they are accidentally stranded out of water this insulating system is too efficient. The whale can cook inside its own envelope of blubber. And a whale's body is too heavy to be out of the water. Its lungs are crushed by its own giant weight.

WHALING

Whaling in Antarctica was a big international industry. Whalers started coming with small fast steamships and the lethal harpoon gun at the end of last century. Whaling stations were built from 1904 in protected harbours on the islands. Then big factory ships arrived, able to cut up and boil the whales at sea. By the summer of 1929–30 more than two hundred whale catcher boats were feeding whales to over forty Norwegian and British factory ships.

But just as in other parts of the world, too many whales were killed. The first to be overhunted were the humpbacks, the easiest to catch. Then blue whales, the largest and most valuable, practically disappeared. Whalers turned to the smaller fin whales and the sei, until not enough could be found. So they hunted the minke.

We know that since 1920 one million three hundred thousand whales have been killed in the Antarctic for their oil, their meat, or their 'whalebone' – the sieves in the mouths of some species. How many whales are left? It is very difficult to count creatures which move around the world's oceans, mostly under the surface. We don't yet know much about the lives of whales. But everyone agrees the destruction has been enormous. Baleen whales have been reduced to a fraction of their former numbers, except for the minke, which has increased to three-quarters of a million. Whaling has fundamentally changed the balance of food and feeding in Antarctic waters.

Today the whaling stations are rusting and empty. Whale bones lie scattered on Antarctic shores. The schools of whales which used to play around visiting ships are a memory.

Various attempts were made to control whaling in Antarctica. They were not very successful. After much effort species in danger of being wiped out were protected. All commercial whaling was finally halted in 1987 except for minke whales taken every year for 'scientific' purposes. But the argument about whether whales should be harvested for human use continues. The Japanese, for example, claim that whales are fish and should be caught like any other fish. Whale meat sells for high prices in Japan.

WHITE-OUT

In a white-out you lose your sense of up and down, far and near. You stumble up a hill and it's only a little ripple in the snow. You fall down a hollow but the surface looks smooth. You see a large tractor in the distance and it's only a tin of fuel.

Everything is the same flat, light, blank, bright whiteness. There are no shadows, no contrasts. You can't tell the difference between snow and sky. You can't see any horizon. White-outs are dangerous and frightening. Planes crash, people get lost and fall over edges. Even birds fly into the ground.

WILKES

The six ships given to Lieutenant Charles Wilkes for the United States Exploring Expedition in 1838 were not at all suitable for exploring in ice. One sank. One was sent home early. One was sold. One crashed into an iceberg. Wilkes was criticized as a leader when he got back home in 1842, and his discoveries were disbelieved. But he achieved a great deal in the Antarctic, as well as much useful scientific and exploring work in the Pacific.

In January and February 1840 Wilkes sailed along the edge of the pack ice for two thousand three hundred kilometres seeing land in the distance many times. He believed that he had discovered the mainland of an Antarctic continent. Some of the land he said he saw turned out not to be there. But the land he did discover is now called Wilkes Land.

The French ships of Dumont d'Urville and the American ships of Charles Wilkes both saw the part of Antarctica which is south of Australia. Each discovered different sections at almost exactly the same time. An American ship even met the French ships. But here, in the loneliest sea in the world, they didn't stop to greet each other.

WIND

Antarctica is the windiest country on Earth. The winds are dry and cold. But some are different from anywhere else. Cold air flowing off the high ice plateau sweeps down the coastal slopes in fierce, raging winds (called 'katabatic', which means 'down-flowing'). The winds vary, stopping and starting suddenly, worse in some places, leaving other places calm.

The first people to experience these terrible violent winds were appalled. The winds blew hurricane force. They broke all known records. Without realizing it the Australians chose what turned out to be the windiest part of the continent for their base at Commonwealth Bay, in 1911. At first men crawled on all fours to stop being picked up and hurled through the air. Then they learnt to 'wind walk', leaning at an angle and bracing against every piece of ice and rock. But when the wind reached one hundred and forty-five to one hundred and sixty kilometres per hour they wriggled on their stomachs.

On Inexpressible Island in winter 1912 the wind blew continually, in tremendous gusts. 'We struggled along with all our strength,' said Raymond Priestley. 'Suddenly it would stop, and we fell forwards on our faces, all our bones jarring on the hard ground. Sometimes we were blown over on our backs. We could only lie there, shaking our fists at the wind, with tears of rage in our eyes, our minds seething with anger. Battling against the fury of the wind nearly drove us mad.'

WINGLESS MIDGE

The largest permanent inhabitant on the Antarctic continent is a mighty (for Antarctica) midge which has no wings. *Belgica Antarctica* can grow up to twelve millimetres long.

WINTER

Today when bases are well-equipped and heated it is possible almost to forget the winter outside. But in the past men dreaded the cold dark months. They tried various ways of coping. It was easy to get on each others' nerves crammed together in small buildings, or on board a ship. On Scott's 1910–12 expedition twenty-five men lived in a hut 7.6m × 15m at Cape Evans. Shackleton's hut at Cape Royds was 5.8m × 10m for fifteen men.

Routines were set up – meals at certain times, singing and concerts on Saturday nights, church service and hymn singing on Sundays, special feasts and games for birthdays. On British expeditions men gave lectures, performed plays, made models, played games, wrote and published magazines, and even published Antarctica's first book, *Aurora Australis*, printed on a small hand press in Shackleton's hut in 1907. The few books brought south were read, the few records played over and over again. A player piano was dragged off Scott's ship *Terra Nova* in 1910 and squeezed into the hut. Men wrote their diaries, did scientific work, looked after the animals, read and reread their letters from home, argued, smoked, talked, fell silent, and made plans for the spring, when the light would come back, and they could set off on expeditions. Always there was work to do preparing for the sledging season ahead: mending clothes, weighing and bagging food into weekly rations, repairing sleeping bags, tents, dog harnesses, and making pieces of equipment.

Nothing could be done without artificial light. All heating, cooking, and water-making required fuel. There was often not enough. During the second winter of Scott's expedition in 1901–4 each man living on board the *Discovery* had to make do with three-quarters of a candle a day. Ice grew under the bunks and had to be chipped off; clothes and bedding were always damp.

The amount of darkness depended on how far south men were from the Antarctic Circle. At Cape Evans, Ross Island, the sun set properly for the first time on 24 February. It disappeared for good on 24 April. But even after the sun had sunk below the horizon for the winter there was beautiful colour in the sky. This was followed by a strange time of twilight, with sea, sky, and ice soft colours of blue-grey, pink and amber. Then came the darkness. Moonlight and starlight glittered off the ice. The aurorae rolled and shifted through the heavens. But the colours of sunlight were gone. Blizzards blew. Temperatures fell to the minus 50s.

Then gradually, a kind of twilight grew around midday, and more could be seen. The sky glowed vivid crimson in the north, where the sun would rise, shading up to light green then deep blue. The light strengthened, lasting longer, until finally the wonderful day so long waited for arrived.

'Half an hour before noon Captain Scott invited me . . . to witness the first sunrise of the season,' wrote Herbert Ponting, 26 August 1911. 'We walked out to the icebergs, climbed to the summit of one . . . and breathlessly waited . . . Within a few minutes a flame seemed to burst from the . . . ridge above Cape Barne; then the upper rim of the sun crept out, not rising but sidling along the slope. A few minutes more, and the blazing orb had cleared the land, and for the first time in more than four months we were bathed in his grateful rays. The world was once more golden. It was one of the moments of our lives, and we could not restrain our joy . . . We felt like boys again, and acted, too, like boys. We shouted and sang for pure delight, and cheered and cheered again. Had we been on a more secure footing I believe we should have danced.'

'It was exciting to get my shadow back,' said one of the scientists.

WOMEN

The Antarctic is a place where saying 'men' instead of 'people' is correct – at least until 1935 when the first woman set foot on the continent. Many men enjoyed the 'all male' life on bases and did not want women included. Now women work in Antarctica in every kind of job, although they are in a minority.

Argentina and Chile send families to live at their bases on islands off the Antarctic Peninsula. The first human baby in the Antarctic region was born on Seymour Island in 1978.

WORKING IN ANTARCTICA

Every year thousands of men and women apply to work in Antarctica as cooks, radio operators, divers, biologists, atmospheric scientists, geologists, mechanics, doctors. Each person who is selected has to be tested physically and psychologically. Living in lonely tough conditions with few companions means only certain kinds of people are suitable.

Some people work in Antarctica for two years at a time. Many go to Antarctica just for the few weeks of summer. Work might be at a base station, or camping out on the ice, in the mountains, or the dry valleys.

The people chosen to work in Antarctica usually train in survival techniques before leaving for the south. Antarctica is beautiful, but dangerous.

WORLD PARK

Some of the world's people believe that they own parts of Antarctica. Some believe it should belong to all the world. Some governments believe Antarctic resources are there for the taking. Other governments believe Antarctica is too vulnerable, and fragile, to use.

Everyone agrees that Antarctica needs protecting. But can anyone agree how?

One suggestion is to declare Antarctica a World Park, for ever. Only scientific research would be allowed. Antarctica would be kept free from international competition. It would be preserved as a wilderness now, and for the future, a place to visit, and wonder at.

The Antarctic Treaty nations agreed in 1991, the thirtieth anniversary of the Treaty, to designate Antarctica 'as a natural reserve devoted to peace and science'.

INDEX